Ellyn Kaschak
Editor

Intimate Betrayal: Domestic Violence in Lesbian Relationships

Intimate Betrayal: Domestic Violence in Lesbian Relationships has been co-published simultaneously as *Women & Therapy*, Volume 23, Number 3 2001.

Pre-publication REVIEWS, COMMENTARIES, EVALUATIONS . . .

" A GROUNDBREAKING EXAMINATION OF A TABOO AND COMPLEX SUBJECT. Both scholarly and down to earth, this superbly edited volume is an indeispensable resource for clinicians, researchers, and lesbians caught up in the cycle of domestic violence."

Dr. Marny Hall
Psychotherapist; Author of The Lesbian Love Companion, *Co-Author of* Queer Blues

More pre-publication
REVIEWS, COMMENTARIES, EVALUATIONS . . .

"RICH . . . explores a complex, painful, and understudied phenomenon among scholars of lesbian issues. THOUGHT PROVOKING, WELL WRITTEN AND INFORMATIVE. Individual, couples and family therapist will find this book extremely useful, as will scholars. . . . An important contribution to the study of domestic violence. . . . An excellent resource for training programs in professional mental health across disciplines as well as courses in women's studies and gender. I HIGHLY RECOMMEND IT."

Beverly Greene, PhD, ABPP
Professor of Psychology
St. John's University, New York

"AN IMPORTANT BOOK that will have a mjaor impact on the field of lesbian studies. The chapters include a review of strategies to prevent domestic abuse among lesbians, the link between domestic abuse and homophobia, feminist models of lesbian battering, responses of feminist counselors to abuse in lesbian relationships. . . . THIS BOOK WILL DO MUCH TO END THE SILENCE ABOUT LESBIAN DOMESTIC VIOLENCE!"

Esther Rothblum, PhD
Professor, University of Vermont
Editor, Journal of Lesbian Studies

The Haworth Press, Inc.

Intimate Betrayal:
Domestic Violence
in Lesbian Relationships

Intimate Betrayal: Domestic Violence in Lesbian Relationships has been co-published simultaneously as *Women & Therapy*, Volume 23, Number 3 2001.

The *Women & Therapy* Monographic "Separates"

Below is a list of "separates," which in serials librarianship means a special issue simultaneously published as a special journal issue or double-issue *and* as a "separate" hardbound monograph. (This is a format which we also call a "DocuSerial.")

"Separates" are published because specialized libraries or professionals may wish to purchase a specific thematic issue by itself in a format which can be separately cataloged and shelved, as opposed to purchasing the journal on an on-going basis. Faculty members may also more easily consider a "separate" for classroom adoption.

"Separates" are carefully classified separately with the major book jobbers so that the journal tie-in can be noted on new book order slips to avoid duplicate purchasing.

You may wish to visit Haworth's website at . . .

http://www.HaworthPress.com

. . . to search our online catalog for complete tables of contents of these separates and related publications.

You may also call 1-800-HAWORTH (outside US/Canada: 607-722-5857), or Fax 1-800-895-0582 (outside US/Canada: 607-771-0012), or e-mail at:

getinfo@haworthpressinc.com

Intimate Betrayal: Domestic Violence in Lesbian Relationships, edited by Ellyn Kaschak, PhD (Vol. 23, No. 3, 2001). *"A groundbreaking examination of a taboo and complex subject. Both scholarly and down to earth, this superbly edited volume is an indispensable resource for clinicians, researchers, and lesbians caught up in the cycle of domestic violence." (Dr. Marny Hall, Psychotherapist; Author of* The Lesbian Love Companion, *Co-Author of* Queer Blues)

The Next Generation: Third Wave Feminist Psychotherapy, edited by Ellyn Kaschak, PhD (Vol. 23, No. 2, 2001). *Discusses the issues young feminists face, focusing on the implications for psychotherapists of the false sense that feminism is no longer necessary.*

Minding the Body: Psychotherapy in Cases of Chronic and Life-Threatening Illness, edited by Ellyn Kaschak, PhD (Vol. 23, No. 1, 2001). *Being diagnosed with cancer, lupus, or fibromyalgia is a traumatic event. All too often, women are told their disease is 'all in their heads' and therefore both 'unreal and insignificant' by a medical profession that dismisses emotions and scorns mental illness. Combining personal narratives and theoretical views of illness,* Minding the Body *offers an alternative approach to the mind-body connection. This book shows the reader how to deal with the painful and difficult emotions that exacerbate illness, while learning the emotional and spiritual lessons illness can teach.*

For Love or Money: The Fee in Feminist Therapy, edited by Marcia Hill, EdD, and Ellyn Kaschak, PhD (Vol. 22, No. 3, 1999). *"Recommended reading for both new and seasoned professionals . . . . An exciting and timely book about 'the last taboo' . . . . " (Carolyn C. Larsen, PhD, Senior Counsellor Emeritus, University of Calgary; Partner, Alberta Psychological Resources Ltd., Calgary, and Co-editor,* Ethical Decision Making in Therapy: Feminist Perspectives)

Beyond the Rule Book: Moral Issues and Dilemmas in the Practice of Psychotherapy, edited by Ellyn Kaschak, PhD, and Marcia Hill, EdD (Vol. 22, No. 2, 1999). *"The authors in this important and timely book tackle the difficult task of working through . . . conflicts, sharing their moral struggles and real life solutions in working with diverse populations and in a variety of clinical settings. . . . Will provide psychotherapists with a thought-provoking source for the stimulating and essential discussion of our own and our profession's moral bases." (Carolyn C. Larsen, PhD, Senior Counsellor Emeritus, University of Calgary, Partner in private practice, Alberta Psychological Resources Ltd., Calgary, and Co-editor,* Ethical Decision Making in Therapy: Feminist Perspectives)

Assault on the Soul: Women in the Former Yugoslavia, edited by Sara Sharratt, PhD, and Ellyn Kaschak, PhD (Vol. 22, No. 1, 1999). *Explores the applications and intersections of feminist therapy, activism and jurisprudence with women and children in the former Yugoslavia.*

Learning from Our Mistakes: Difficulties and Failures in Feminist Therapy, edited by Marcia Hill, EdD, and Esther D. Rothblum, PhD (Vol. 21, No. 3, 1998). *"A courageous and fundamental step in evolving a well-grounded body of theory and of investigating the assumptions that unexamined, lead us to error." (Teresa Bernardez, MD, Training and Supervising Analyst, The Michigan Psychoanalytic Council)*

Feminist Therapy as a Political Act, edited by Marcia Hill, EdD (Vol. 21, No. 2, 1998). *"A real contribution to the field. . . . A valuable tool for feminist therapists and those who want to learn about feminist therapy." (Florence L. Denmark, PhD, Robert S. Pace Distinguished Professor of Psychology and Chair, Psychology Department, Pace University, New York, New York)*

Breaking the Rules: Women in Prison and Feminist Therapy, edited by Judy Harden, PhD, and Marcia Hill, EdD (Vol. 20, No. 4 & Vol. 21, No. 1, 1998). *"Fills a long-recognized gap in the psychology of women curricula, demonstrating that feminist theory can be made relevant to the practice of feminism, even in prison." (Suzanne J. Kessler, PhD, Professor of Psychology and Women's Studies, State University of New York at Purchase)*

Children's Rights, Therapists' Responsibilities: Feminist Commentaries, edited by Gail Anderson, MA, and Marcia Hill, EdD (Vol. 20, No. 2, 1997). *"Addresses specific practice dimensions that will help therapists organize and resolve conflicts about working with children, adolescents, and their families in therapy." (Feminist Bookstore News)*

More than a Mirror: How Clients Influence Therapists' Lives, edited by Marcia Hill, EdD (Vol. 20, No. 1, 1997). *"Courageous, insightful, and deeply moving. These pages reveal the scrupulous self-examination and self-reflection of conscientious therapists at their best. An important contribution to feminist therapy literature and a book worth reading by therapists and clients alike." (Rachel Josefowitz Siegal, MSW, retired feminist therapy practitioner; Co-Editor, Women Changing Therapy; Jewish Women in Therapy; and Celebrating the Lives of Jewish Women: Patterns in a Feminist Sampler)*

Sexualities, edited by Marny Hall, PhD, LCSW (Vol. 19, No. 4, 1997). *"Explores the diverse and multifaceted nature of female sexuality, covering topics including sadomasochism in the therapy room, sexual exploitation in cults, and genderbending in cyberspace." (Feminist Bookstore News)*

Couples Therapy: Feminist Perspectives, edited by Marcia Hill, EdD, and Esther D. Rothblum, PhD (Vol. 19, No. 3, 1996). *Addresses some of the inadequacies, omissions, and assumptions in traditional couples' therapy to help you face the issues of race, ethnicity, and sexual orientation in helping couples today.*

A Feminist Clinician's Guide to the Memory Debate, edited by Susan Contratto, PhD, and M. Janice Gutfreund, PhD (Vol. 19, No. 1, 1996). *"Unites diverse scholars, clinicians, and activists in an insightful and useful examination of the issues related to recovered memories." (Feminist Bookstore News)*

Classism and Feminist Therapy: Counting Costs, edited by Marcia Hill, EdD, and Esther D. Rothblum, PhD (Vol. 18, No. 3/4, 1996). *"Educates, challenges, and questions the influence of classism on the clinical practice of psychotherapy with women." (Kathleen P. Gates, MA, Certified Professional Counselor, Center for Psychological Health, Superior, Wisconsin)*

Lesbian Therapists and Their Therapy: From Both Sides of the Couch, edited by Nancy D. Davis, MD, Ellen Cole, PhD, and Esther D. Rothblum, PhD (Vol. 18, No. 2, 1996). *"Highlights the power and boundary issues of psychotherapy from perspectives that many readers may have neither considered nor experienced in their own professional lives." (Psychiatric Services)*

Feminist Foremothers in Women's Studies, Psychology, and Mental Health, edited by Phyllis Chesler, PhD, Esther D. Rothblum, PhD, and Ellen Cole, PhD (Vol. 17, No. 1/2/3/4, 1995). *"A must for feminist scholars and teachers . . . These women's personal experiences are poignant and powerful." (Women's Studies International Forum)*

Women's Spirituality, Women's Lives, edited by Judith Ochshorn, PhD, and Ellen Cole, PhD (Vol. 16, No. 2/3, 1995). *"A delightful and complex book on spirituality and sacredness in women's lives." (Joan Clingan, MA, Spiritual Psychology, Graduate Advisor, Prescott College Master of Arts Program)*

Psychopharmacology from a Feminist Perspective, edited by Jean A. Hamilton, MD, Margaret Jensvold, MD, Esther D. Rothblum, PhD, and Ellen Cole, PhD (Vol. 16, No. 1, 1995). *"Challenges readers to increase their sensitivity and awareness of the role of sex and gender in response to and acceptance of pharmacologic therapy." (American Journal of Pharmaceutical Education)*

Wilderness Therapy for Women: The Power of Adventure, edited by Ellen Cole, PhD, Esther D. Rothblum, PhD, and Eve Erdman, MEd, MLS (Vol. 15, No. 3/4, 1994). *"There's an undeniable excitement in these pages about the thrilling satisfaction of meeting challenges in the physical world, the world outside our cities that is unfamiliar, uneasy territory for many women. If you're interested at all in the subject, this book is well worth your time." (Psychology of Women Quarterly)*

Bringing Ethics Alive: Feminist Ethics in Psychotherapy Practice, edited by Nanette K. Gartrell, MD (Vol. 15, No. 1, 1994). *"Examines the theoretical and practical issues of ethics in feminist therapies. From the responsibilities of training programs to include social issues ranging from racism to sexism to practice ethics, this outlines real questions and concerns." (Midwest Book Review)*

Women with Disabilities: Found Voices, edited by Mary Willmuth, PhD, and Lillian Holcomb, PhD (Vol. 14, No. 3/4, 1994). *"These powerful chapters often jolt the anti-disability consciousness and force readers to contend with the ways in which disability has been constructed, disguised, and rendered disgusting by much of society."* (Academic Library Book Review)

Faces of Women and Aging, edited by Nancy D. Davis, MD, Ellen Cole, PhD, and Esther D. Rothblum, PhD (Vol. 14, No. 1/2, 1993). *"This uplifting, helpful book is of great value not only for aging women, but also for women of all ages who are interested in taking active control of their own lives." (New Mature Woman)*

Refugee Women and Their Mental Health: Shattered Societies, Shattered Lives, edited by Ellen Cole, PhD, Oliva M. Espin, PhD, and Esther D. Rothblum, PhD (Vol. 13, No. 1/2/3, 1992). *"The ideas presented are rich and the perspectives varied, and the book is an important contribution to understanding refugee women in a global context." (Comtemporary Psychology)*

Women, Girls and Psychotherapy: Reframing Resistance, edited by Carol Gilligan, PhD, Annie Rogers, PhD, and Deborah Tolman, EdD (Vol. 11, No. 3/4, 1991). *"Of use to educators, psychotherapists, and parents–in short, to any person who is directly involved with girls at adolescence." (Harvard Educational Review)*

Professional Training for Feminist Therapists: Personal Memoirs, edited by Esther D. Rothblum, PhD, and Ellen Cole, PhD (Vol. 11, No. 1, 1991). *"Exciting, interesting, and filled with the angst and the energies that directed these women to develop an entirely different approach to counseling." (Science Books & Films)*

Jewish Women in Therapy: Seen But Not Heard, edited by Rachel Josefowitz Siegel, MSW, and Ellen Cole, PhD (Vol. 10, No. 4, 1991). *"A varied collection of prose and poetry, first-person stories, and accessible theoretical pieces that can help Jews and non-Jews, women and men, therapists and patients, and general readers to grapple with questions of Jewish women's identities and diversity." (Canadian Psychology)*

Women's Mental Health in Africa, edited by Esther D. Rothblum, PhD, and Ellen Cole, PhD (Vol. 10, No. 3, 1990). *"A valuable contribution and will be of particular interest to scholars in women's studies, mental health, and cross-cultural psychology." (Contemporary Psychology)*

Motherhood: A Feminist Perspective, edited by Jane Price Knowles, MD, and Ellen Cole, PhD (Vol. 10, No. 1/2, 1990). *"Provides some enlightening perspectives. . . . It is worth the time of both male and female readers." (Comtemporary Psychology)*

Diversity and Complexity in Feminist Therapy, edited by Laura Brown, PhD, ABPP, and Maria P. P. Root, PhD (Vol. 9, No. 1/2, 1990). *"A most convincing discussion and illustration of the importance of adopting a multicultural perspective for theory building in feminist therapy. . . . This book is a must for therapists and should be included on psychology of women syllabi." (Association for Women in Psychology Newsletter)*

Fat Oppression and Psychotherapy, edited by Laura S. Brown, PhD, and Esther D. Rothblum, PhD (Vol. 8, No. 3, 1990). *"Challenges many traditional beliefs about being fat . . . A refreshing new perspective for approaching and thinking about issues related to weight." (Association for Women in Psychology Newsletter)*

Lesbianism: Affirming Nontraditional Roles, edited by Esther D. Rothblum, PhD, and Ellen Cole, PhD (Vol. 8, No. 1/2, 1989). *"Touches on many of the most significant issues brought before therapists today." (Newsletter of the Association of Gay & Lesbian Psychiatrists)*

Women and Sex Therapy: Closing the Circle of Sexual Knowledge, edited by Ellen Cole, PhD, and Esther D. Rothblum, PhD (Vol. 7, No. 2/3, 1989). *"Adds immeasureably to the feminist therapy literature that dispels male paradigms of pathology with regard to women." (Journal of Sex Education & Therapy)*

The Politics of Race and Gender in Therapy, edited by Lenora Fulani, PhD (Vol. 6, No. 4, 1988). *Women of color examine newer therapies that encourage them to develop their historical identity.*

Treating Women's Fear of Failure, edited by Esther D. Rothblum, PhD, and Ellen Cole, PhD (Vol. 6, No. 3, 1988). *"Should be recommended reading for all mental health professionals, social workers, educators, and vocational counselors who work with women." (The Journal of Clinical Psychiatry)*

Women, Power, and Therapy: Issues for Women, edited by Marjorie Braude, MD (Vol. 6, No. 1/2, 1987). *"Raise[s] therapists' consciousness about the importance of considering gender-based power in therapy. . . welcome contribution." (Australian Journal of Psychology)*

Dynamics of Feminist Therapy, edited by Doris Howard (Vol. 5, No. 2/3, 1987). *"A comprehensive treatment of an important and vexing subject." (Australian Journal of Sex, Marriage and Family)*

A Woman's Recovery from the Trauma of War: Twelve Responses from Feminist Therapists and Activists, edited by Esther D. Rothblum, PhD, and Ellen Cole, PhD (Vol. 5, No. 1, 1986). *"A milestone. In it, twelve women pay very close attention to a woman who has been deeply wounded by war." (The World)*

Women and Mental Health: New Directions for Change, edited by Carol T. Mowbray, PhD, Susan Lanir, MA, and Marilyn Hulce, MSW, ACSW (Vol. 3, No. 3/4, 1985). *"The overview of sex differences in disorders is clear and sensitive, as is the review of sexual exploitation of clients by therapists. . . . Mandatory reading for all therapists who work with women." (British Journal of Medical Psychology and The British Psychological Society)*

Women Changing Therapy: New Assessments, Values, and Strategies in Feminist Therapy, edited by Joan Hamerman Robbins and Rachel Josefowitz Siegel, MSW (Vol. 2, No. 2/3, 1983). *"An excellent collection to use in teaching therapists that reflection and resolution in treatment do not simply lead to adaptation, but to an active inner process of judging." (News for Women in Psychiatry)*

Current Feminist Issues in Psychotherapy, edited by The New England Association for Women in Psychology (Vol. 1, No. 3, 1983). *Addresses depression, displaced homemakers, sibling incest, and body image from a feminist perspective.*

Intimate Betrayal: Domestic Violence in Lesbian Relationships

Ellyn Kaschak, PhD
Editor

Intimate Betrayal: Domestic Violence in Lesbian Relationships has been co-published simultaneously as *Women & Therapy*, Volume 23, Number 3 2001.

The Haworth Press, Inc.
New York • London • Oxford

284392

Intimate Betrayal: Domestic Violence in Lesbian Relationships has been co-published simultaneously as *Women & Therapy*™, Volume 23, Number 3 2001.

The development, preparation, and publication of this work has been undertaken with great care. However, the publisher, employees, editors, and agents of The Haworth Press and all imprints of The Haworth Press, Inc., including The Haworth Medical Press® and Pharmaceutical Products Press®, are not responsible for any errors contained herein or for consequences that may ensue from use of materials or information contained in this work. Opinions expressed by the author(s) are not necessarily those of The Haworth Press, Inc.

Cover design by Thomas J. Mayshock Jr.

Library of Congress Cataloging-in-Publication Data

Intimate betrayal : domestic violence in lesbian relationships / Ellyn Kaschak, editor.
    p. cm.
    Published also as v. 23, no. 3, 2001 of Women & therapy.
    Includes bibliographical references and index.
    ISBN 0-7890-1662-1 (alk. paper) – ISBN 0-7890-1663-X (alk. paper)
  1. Abused lesbians. 2. Lesbian couples. 3. Family violence. I. Kaschak, Ellyn, 1943- II. Women & therapy.
HQ75.5 .I575 2001
362.83′92–dc21

2001039832

Indexing, Abstracting & Website/Internet Coverage

This section provides you with a list of major indexing & abstracting services. That is to say, each service began covering this periodical during the year noted in the right column. Most Websites which are listed below have indicated that they will either post, disseminate, compile, archive, cite or alert their own Website users with research-based content from this work. (This list is as current as the copyright date of this publication.)

Abstracting, Website/Indexing Coverage . . . . Year When Coverage Began

- *Academic Abstracts/CD-ROM* **1995**
- *Academic ASAP <www.galegroup.com>* **1992**
- *Academic Index (on-line)* **1992**
- *Academic Search Elite (EBSCO)* **1994**
- *Alternative Press Index (online & CD-ROM from NISC)*
    <www.nisc.com> **1982**
- *Behavioral Medicine Abstracts* **1996**
- *BUBL Information Service, an Internet-based Information*
    Service for the UK higher education community
    <URL: http://bubl.ac.uk/> **1995**
- *Child Development Abstracts & Bibliography (in print & online)* **1994**
- *CINAHL (Cumulative Index to Nursing & Allied Health*
    Literature) **2000**
- *CNPIEC Reference Guide: Chinese National Directory*
    of Foreign Periodicals **1996**
- *Contemporary Women's Issues* **1998**
- *Current Contents: Social & Behavioral Sciences*
    <www.isinet.com> **1995**

(continued)

(continued)

Special Bibliographic Notes related to special journal issues (separates) and indexing/abstracting:

- indexing/abstracting services in this list will also cover material in any "separate" that is co-published simultaneously with Haworth's special thematic journal issue or DocuSerial. Indexing/abstracting usually covers material at the article/chapter level.
- monographic co-editions are intended for either non-subscribers or libraries which intend to purchase a second copy for their circulating collections.
- monographic co-editions are reported to all jobbers/wholesalers/approval plans. The source journal is listed as the "series" to assist the prevention of duplicate purchasing in the same manner utilized for books-in-series.
- to facilitate user/access services all indexing/abstracting services are encouraged to utilize the co-indexing entry note indicated at the bottom of the first page of each article/chapter/contribution.
- this is intended to assist a library user of any reference tool (whether print, electronic, online, or CD-ROM) to locate the monographic version if the library has purchased this version but not a subscription to the source journal.
- individual articles/chapters in any Haworth publication are also available through the Haworth Document Delivery Service (HDDS).

ABOUT THE EDITOR

Ellyn Kaschak, PhD, is Professor of Psychology at San Jose State University in San Jose, California. She is author of *Engendered Lives: A New Psychology of Women's Experience*, as well as numerous articles and chapters on feminist psychology and psychotherapy. Dr. Kaschak is editor of *Minding the Body: Psychotherapy in Cases of Chronic and Life-Threatening Illness* and *The Next Generation: Third Wave Feminist Psychotherapy*, and co-editor of *Assault on the Soul: Women in the Former Yugoslavia*; *Beyond the Rule Book: Moral Issues and Dilemmas in the Practice of Psychotherapy*, and *For Love or Money: The Fee in Feminist Therapy*. She has had more than thirty years of experience practicing psychotherapy, is past Chair of the Feminist Therapy Institute and of the APA Committee on Women and is Fellow of Division 35, the Psychology of Women, Division 12, Clinical Psychology, Division 45, Ethnic Minority Issues and Division 52, International Psychology, of the American Psychological Association. She is co-editor of the journal *Women & Therapy*.

Intimate Betrayal: Domestic Violence in Lesbian Relationships

CONTENTS

Intimate Betrayal:
Domestic Violence
in Lesbian Relationships

Ellyn Kaschak

My heart is convulsed within me; terrors of death assail me . . . I said,
O that I had the wings of a dove! I would fly away and find rest; . . . It is
not an enemy who reviles me . . . I could bear that; . . . but it is you, my
equal, my companion, my friend . . .

55th Psalm

Early feminist psychology had the dubious distinction, the sad responsibility of uncovering the many forms of violence and abuse against women and children that reside within the bounds of intimate relationships. Feminist researchers and clinicians were also responsible for the initial development of successful and powerful treatment protocols for intimate partner violence, many of which are now accepted as standard practice by mental health professionals, as well as legal and judicial systems.

These analyses are based, in large part, on understanding the malignant effects of patriarchal power and male privilege and the trauma and injury inflicted upon the less powerful, including partners in heterosexual relationships. However, within the last decade or so, it has become increasingly apparent that intimate forms of violence also occur within lesbian relationships, as well as between gay males, where the power differential implied by gender differ-

[Haworth co-indexing entry note]: "Intimate Betrayal: Domestic Violence in Lesbian Relationships." Kaschak, Ellyn. Co-published simultaneously in *Women & Therapy* (The Haworth Press, Inc.) Vol. 23, No. 3, 2001, pp. 1-5; and: *Intimate Betrayal: Domestic Violence in Lesbian Relationships* (ed: Ellyn Kaschak) The Haworth Press, Inc., 2001, pp. 1-5. Single or multiple copies of this article are available for a fee from The Haworth Document Delivery Service [1-800-342-9678, 9:00 a.m. - 5:00 p.m. (EST). E-mail address: getinfo@haworthpressinc.com].

1

ences alone is not present. Paula Poorman, in her article, provides a broad and thorough introduction to this literature.

It has been difficult for many members of the lesbian community and feminists, whether lesbian or not, to accept that there are among us women who batter and abuse other women. Yet, unfortunately, they exist in large enough numbers to require the systematic attention of researchers and therapists alike. The existence of violence in lesbian relationships calls into question some of the most accepted explanations for intimate violence and highlights the necessity for developing models of intervention that are appropriate and effective in the circumstance of a relationship between women, ones that take into consideration both the similarities to and differences from violence in intimate heterosexual and in gay male relationships.

For example, our well-accepted analyses of violence based in male privilege and power may seem irrelevant or inapplicable to lesbians. Yet while neither partner in a lesbian relationship enjoys male privilege and power, we all live in a society that promotes hierarchy, power differential, inequality and, yes, violence. These are endemic to patriarchy and why should they not find their way into relationships lived in this cultural milieu? Additionally, lesbian relationships are directly influenced by other societal power inequities that impact all citizens, including sexism, and those based in class, race, ethnic, and economic inequality, as well as interpersonal differences in power. The interface of these forces is considered in the work of Janice Ristock. Tragically it is no longer surprising, although it may still be shocking, to learn that women physically abuse their own children and we must also add to this list that adult women, in percentages comparable to those within heterosexual relationships, batter their partners.

Of course, the differential impact of homophobia and heterosexism on lesbian relationships must also be taken into account. Kimberly Balsam, Janice Ristock and Leanne Tigert identify these influences as crucial and explore some of their consequences, while raising questions for future investigation. As one example, the existence of violence and hatred toward lesbians and gays in society affects the violence within lesbian and gay relationships. As another, all the complex issues in the lives of most lesbians involving whether and when to "come out" and to whom, and the degree of isolation and/or support of family members and friends differentially impact lesbian relationships.

There are certain unique characteristics of the lesbian community, including ties to the "chosen family," which sometimes replaces the biological one in providing caring, closeness and context. Among the closest bonds may be those with former lovers or partners. As in other circumstances of oppression, these kinds of ties may have developed in adversity to become some of the unique strengths of the lesbian community. We need more information about how they differentially impact the existence of violence, as well as the reporting of violence, and how they can be mobilized effectively in solutions to the problem.

Are the individual characteristics of the male batterer also found in female batterers of their female partners? For example, it would seem a truism to say that anyone who resorts to violence lacks more effective interpersonal skills and instead is exercising coercion and control. Diane H. Miller, Kathryn Greene, Vickie Causby, Barbara W. White and Lettie L. Lockhart found different personality and relational variables related to the degree of aggression, including self-esteem, degree of independence, fusion and control.

Is the cyclical model of abuse so frequently applied to heterosexual relationships applicable in lesbian relationships? The answer may be some of the time and this may also be so in heterosexual and gay male relationships. For example and somewhat ironically, the cycle of abuse within a particular relationship is predicated upon a certain amount of responsibility and honesty on the part of the batterer. That is, she must, at some point, acknowledge her own violence and, in some manner direct or indirect, express regret. What of those who experience no regret, who continue to blame their partners and who will not be held accountable? Absent truth and accountability, there can be no apology, no honeymoon period. Where there is not truth there can be no cycle. Perpetrators who continue consistently to lie and to deny responsibility should be studied along with those who periodically accept even limited responsibility.

Even for other members of the lesbian community, it can be difficult to believe that lesbians batter, as Kimberly Balsam points out. Erin McLaughlin and Patricia Rozee actually found that members of the lesbian community were more familiar with explanations for heterosexual domestic violence. The abused partner can be disbelieved, be pressured to maintain privacy, deal with the issue only in therapy or remain silent. While feminists early on declared that the personal is political, in this case the personal is often kept personal. What occurs between two lesbian partners in the privacy of their own home is often considered the purview of the two or of their therapy.

The different meanings and consequences for a lesbian of calling the police or speaking publicly about the abuse when she may not be comfortable or safe being public about being a lesbian must be considered and respected. Anything less subjects these women to the secondary trauma of being misunderstood, shamed, blamed or even endangered. Psychologists and mental health workers, police officers and jurists must be educated and sensitive to the complex issues in the lives of lesbians.

Should the injured woman choose to speak outside of the privacy of the therapeutic hour, she may be shunned or shamed. Breaking the silence and violating the frequent demands for secrecy imposed by partners, self or the community can be seen as an act of aggression toward the perpetrator and this perception can be shared by the lesbian community. As one batterer stated to her partner, who had finally told the story to a few mutual friends, "I wounded you in private and now you have wounded me in public. We are even." Several of the friends agreed.

This must stop. Any woman who is abused and traumatized must be helped to heal and this very healing requires the acknowledgement of the professions and of the community that she has been wronged and deserves a fair hearing.

Yet lesbian battering is not only a psychological issue, not only a cultural issue and not only a political issue. It is, at the very same time, a moral issue. The violent partner must be held solely and completely accountable for her violence no matter her protestations that she was provoked and no matter whether or not she was provoked. She is the one who ultimately chose violence over and over. Had she been horrified at the first instance and immediately stopped with whatever means or support necessary, then the violence would not have developed into the pattern that we name battering.

This offense is an offense against one woman at a time, but also against the entire community and particularly against the lesbian community. It is an individual act of violence, but it is not only that. Thus, the offender must eventually make amends on all these levels. The network of relationships within the lesbian community is unique in many ways and might provide an ideal circumstance for developing community forms of healing and reconciliation. I propose, as I have in other circumstances of abuse, violence, and injustice, that we take a close look at the model of the Truth and Reconciliation Courts of South Africa and other forms of witnessing and reconciliation that are being practiced in Israel, Palestine and elsewhere. Community interventions are as powerful, or more powerful, than private therapeutic ones for the very reason that they are not private. The injured party is given a fair hearing.

Many excellent community and clinical services are already in place, particularity in larger cities. There are hot lines and services particularly for lesbians. More need to be added in communities that lack specific services for lesbians. Feminist therapy has begun to develop specific approaches, one of which is described in the article by Paula Poorman and Sheila M. Seelau. Leanne Tigert, after exploring the religious roots of shame and homophobia, offers the model of liberation theology. In smaller communities, workers must be trained in the specific issues related to abuse in lesbian relationships.

What can any individual, lesbian or not, do? Interrupt victim-blaming. Emphasize that it is not the survivor's fault. Keep attention on the abuser. What else can professionals and the community do? Speak about abuse, provide education and create an environment which not only permits, but encourages, those being injured to come forward.

The entire community must be educated, must be disabused of their incorrect and biased ideas about this practice. The lesbian community must refuse the privacy that allows the perpetrator to continue unimpeded and places the entire demand of truth on the shoulders of the abused and traumatized woman. In part, batterers abuse because they can.

Forging Community Links
to Address Abuse
in Lesbian Relationships

Paula B. Poorman

SUMMARY. This study is a comprehensive review of lesbian domestic abuse in the psychological, sociological, legal, and social work literature. Planning intervention and prevention strategies is discussed in light of what is known and what remains to be known. A strong argument is made to turn attention away from the elusive tasks of documenting prevalence and incidence characteristics, and forge the community links needed to develop effective intervention and prevention strategies. *[Article copies available for a fee from The Haworth Document Delivery Service: 1-800-342-9678. E-mail address: <getinfo@haworthpressinc.com> Website: <http://www.HaworthPress.com> © 2001 by The Haworth Press, Inc. All rights reserved.]*

KEYWORDS. Lesbian, domestic abuse, intervention, prevention

Paula B. Poorman, PhD, is Assistant Professor, Department of Psychology, University of Wisconsin-Whitewater.

Address correspondence to: Paula B. Poorman, PhD, Department of Psychology, Winther Hall, 800 West Main Street, Whitewater, WI 53190-1790 (E-mail: poormanp@uwwvax.uww.edu).

[Haworth co-indexing entry note]: "Forging Community Links to Address Abuse in Lesbian Relationships." Poorman, Paula B. Co-published simultaneously in *Women & Therapy* (The Haworth Press, Inc.) Vol. 23, No. 3, 2001, pp. 7-24; and: *Intimate Betrayal: Domestic Violence in Lesbian Relationships* (ed: Ellyn Kaschak) The Haworth Press, Inc., 2001, pp. 7-24. Single or multiple copies of this article are available for a fee from The Haworth Document Delivery Service [1-800-342-9678, 9:00 a.m. - 5:00 p.m. (EST). E-mail address: getinfo@haworthpressinc.com].

With the third wave of feminism, the 1960s and 1970s saw the grassroots beginnings of disclosing, and ending the denial and minimization of, men's abuse of the women who were their wives, girlfriends, and lovers (Martin, 1981). As grassroots organizations gained increasing public recognition and funding in the early 1980s, lesbians, already at the forefront of the battered women's movement, began the uneasy task of acknowledging the presence of abuse in lesbian domestic relationships. About the same time, Steinem, in a keynote address to the National Coalition Against Sexual Assault (1983), asked a predominantly heterosexually-identified movement to look to the lesbian community for models of non-violent relationships. This seemed an ideal choice since feminist sociopolitical analysis taught that abuse was the result of a misogynist and patriarchal society and assumed men as abusers and women as victims/survivors. When lesbians began to give voice to observations and experiences of abuse within their own communities, they were revealing paradoxes in that model and analysis, and delivering a message that few wanted to hear. The establishment of the National Coalition Against Domestic Violence Lesbian Task Force and publication of the groundbreaking book *Naming the Violence: Speaking Out About Lesbian Battering* (Lobel, 1986) began to change our understanding of the dynamics of domestic violence.

The last two decades have witnessed increased attention to lesbian domestic abuse in the psychological, sociological, legal, and social work literature. Seminal texts have gathered articles discussing abuse in lesbian relationships from a variety of different perspectives (Elliot, 1990; Lobel, 1986; Renzetti, 1992; Renzetti & Miley, 1996). General texts exploring lesbian issues, lesbian therapy, and domestic abuse have included chapters addressing abuse in lesbian relationships. Still, the literature has remained sparse and particularly insufficient in key areas. The objective of this article is to review the literature of abuse in lesbian relationships, examining not only what is known, but what is missing. Such a review may facilitate efforts to design more effective intervention and prevention strategies.

LITERATURE REVIEW

Articles that address abuse in lesbian relationships can be generally grouped as: (a) empirical estimates of the rates of abuse and descriptive characteristics of the abuse; (b) anecdotal evidence from victims/survivors, abusers, and service providers; (c) calls to address the needs of underserved populations; and (d) descriptions of approaches, practices, services, and community organizing efforts. Each of these has been addressed in turn.

Empirical Estimates and Descriptive Characteristics of Abuse

By far the single largest group of articles within the reviewed literature estimates the rates of abuse in lesbian relationships and describes the character of the abuses. Some works have discussed only lesbian abuse; others have included gay male or heterosexual data, as well. Brand and Kidd (1986) surveyed fifty-five lesbian students recruited through ads and campus groups. Loulan (1987) surveyed a self-selected sample of 1,566 lesbians. Schilit, Lie, and Montagne (1990) surveyed 104 lesbians through an organizational mailing. Coleman (1990) surveyed ninety couples recruited through ads, newsletters, fliers, therapists, support group facilitators, and community organizations, and then extended the sample by snowballing. Lie, Schilit, Bush, Montagne, and Reyes (1991) surveyed 174 lesbians through an organizational mailing. Lie and Gentlewarrior (1991) and Lockhart, White, Causby, and Isaac (1994) surveyed 1,099 and 284 lesbians, respectively, at women's festivals. Renzetti's (1992) *Violent Betrayal: Partner Abuse in Lesbian Relationships* described her recruitment of 100 lesbians by advertising and displaying posters at women's organizations, agencies, bookstores, and bars, placing ads in newspapers and national publications, and sending mailings to lesbian and gay newspapers and more than 1,000 organizations throughout Canada and the United States. Unlike previous studies, the 100 participants who completed Renzetti's four-part questionnaire all identified as victims of abuse. Approximately equal numbers of studies have included surveys or author-created questionnaires completed by both gay men and lesbians (Bologna, Waterman, & Dawson, 1987; Gardner, 1989; Sloan & Edmund, 1996; Waldner-Haugrud, Gratch, & Magruder, 1997) or heterosexual women (Bradford, Ryan, & Rothblum, 1994; Pagelow, 1984) as comparisons to lesbians. Researchers have used recruitment strategies similar to those used in the all-lesbian samples. Their findings are outlined below.

Results: Estimates of prevalence. Estimates of the prevalence of abuse in lesbian relationships have varied widely as studies have not always asked the same questions or measured the same types of abuse. Although Loulan (1987) estimated that abuse affects 17% of lesbians, most studies have reported much higher estimates. Somewhere from 47% (Coleman, 1990) to 52% (Lie & Gentlewarrior, 1991) to 60% (Bologna, Waterman, & Dawson, 1987) to 73% (Lie, Schilit, Bush, Montagne, & Reyes, 1991) of lesbians who responded to questionnaires and surveys have reported experiencing some form of physical, sexual, or emotional-psychological abuse in at least one relationship. A National Coalition of Domestic Violence Programs study conducted in 1997 found 2,352 incidents of violence in lesbian and gay relationships in just the twelve cities that participated (NCAVP, 1998). These numbers cannot be considered true prevalence estimates. Without an accurate count of the lesbian population no ratio of numbers of problems to population can be ascertained. While the estimates must be interpreted with caution, the data have still demonstrated convincingly that abuse occurs in lesbian relationships with sufficient frequency not to be an anomaly.

Results: Incident characteristics. Much of the empirical research has also focused on identifying the forms that abuse takes in lesbian relationships. Abuse in lesbian relationships includes physical abuse; sexual abuse; verbal, emotional, and psychological abuse; threats; and destruction of special or significant property.

Physical abuse is sometimes further categorized as either (a) engaging in physically aggressive acts (e.g., hitting, slapping, wrestling, shoving, grabbing, throwing) or (b) withholding physical necessities (e.g., food, water, shelter, sleep; Poorman, 1986). In lesbian relationships, the most common forms of physical abuse include pushing and shoving, hitting with fists or open hands, scratching or hitting the face, breasts, or genitals, and throwing things at the victim/survivor (Renzetti, 1992).

Sexual abuse is defined as any non-consensual sexual behavior (Poorman, 1986). Over half of the lesbians who participated in research surveys have reported at least one incident of sexual coercion, with penetration the most frequent outcome (Waldner-Haugrud & Gratch, 1997).

Estimates of verbal abuse in lesbian relationships have been as high as 95% (Kelly & Warshafsky, 1987), with the most common forms being verbal threats, being demeaned in front of friends, relatives, and strangers, having sleeping or eating habits interrupted, abusing others in the household like children or pets, which in turn, has inflicted harm on the respondents.

Threats of abuse include any verbal statement intended to intimidate or resulting in intimidating the partner (Poorman, 1986). Those threats unique to lesbians have included outing a partner. As in heterosexual abuse, abuse in lesbian relationships has also included the destruction of special or significant property.

In addition to the most commonly reported forms of abuse, research has documented that survey participants have experienced each type of abuse listed in the Conflict Tactics Scale (Straus, 1979, 1989). Reports of dramatic incidents of stabbing, shooting, and having guns and knives inserted into the partner's vagina have been rare, but still present. Further, lesbian abusers, like heterosexual male abusers, are expert at tailoring abuse to the partner's vulnerabilities (Renzetti, 1992). Examples have included the woman confined to a wheelchair whose partner abandoned her in a dangerous setting without her chair. Another abuser forced her diabetic partner to eat sugar.

Lethality and frequency of abuse. Research has now identified that the abuse that occurs in lesbian relationships is recurrent and tends to grow more severe and lethal with time, as it does in heterosexual relationships. About half of the lesbians who participated in research surveys indicated that they had experienced ten or more abusive incidents during the course of their relationships (54%); about three quarters had experienced six or more (74%; Renzetti, 1992). Close to three quarters of the lesbians who answered questionnaires reported that the abuse grew more severe with each successive incident (71%). The vast majority of the abuse in lesbian relationships, then, has been shown to meet the criteria found in Leeder's typology for what is called "chronic battering and emotional battering relationships" (Leeder, 1988). Chronic battering indicates that physical abuse is recurrent and becomes increasingly lethal, escalating over time. Emotional battering indicates that the verbal or psychological abuse is recurrent, increasingly damaging, and escalates over time (Renzetti, 1997).

Anecdotal Evidence

Anecdotal evidence has brought to life the often dry and desensitizing quantification of academic studies of violence and abuse. The very real victims and abusers, and their very real communities are those who ultimately lose or gain with oppressive or enhanced social services, advocacy, mental health services, and criminal justice responses. Nearly equal to the number of articles describing the nature and number of abuses have been the number of articles that offer a story of abuse in lesbian relationships.

Victims/survivors and service providers have narrated the chronicles of the damage done by the physical, sexual, and psychological-emotional abuse, and the barriers to resolution for lesbians (e.g., Barry, 1990; Crall, 1986; Edgington, 1990; Hurley, 1986; Lisa, 1986; Northwood, 1986). Anger, shame, isolation, self-blame and self-doubt, and confusion as well as strength, courage, and thriving have been brought to life when seen through the eyes of these courageous women. In addition, the anecdotes have offered vivid, individualized accounts of the barriers to effective service provision by therapists, social and community services, and criminal justice systems. Stories of ineffective (e.g., West, 1992), homophobic (e.g., Goldyn, 1981; Marie, 1984), or lethal decisions (e.g., Marie, 1984; Goldfarb, 1996) have documented a frightening picture of abuses within the very systems designed to protect women against abuse. One attorney described her own isolation working at a public defenders office as she addressed the legal issues, heterosexism, and homophobia faced by lesbians abused in relationships (West, 1992). Anecdotes have personalized lives led, abuses survived, effects suffered, and systemic barriers faced. What cannot be known from anecdotal evidence is whether these stories constitute measurable norms or vivid illustrations.

Calls to Address the Needs of Underserved Populations

Although many articles have offered topic-specific reviews of the lesbian abuse literature, four authors stand out. Hart (1986), Kanuha (1990a, 1990b), Waldron (1996), and Coleman (1994) have focused on the needs of populations still underserved by the movement's work to address abuse in lesbian relationships. Hart (1986) and Kanuha (1990a) first warned of the need to include lesbians of color. In a subsequent article, Kanuha (1990b) called lesbians and feminists to task about the unique challenges faced by lesbians of color in violent relationships and discussed the role of racism within lesbian and feminist communities in silencing lesbians of color. Further, she challenged the assumption that heterosexism and homophobia affect all lesbians the same way, pointing out the additional oppression faced not only by lesbians of color, but by those faced by the impact of ageism, classism, anti-Semitism, and ableism. Kanuha confronted the impact of internalized racism, sexism, and homophobia, calling the impact on lesbians of color "triple jeopardy." Just as open acknowledgment of the existence of lesbian abuse threatened to unravel the carefully woven tapestry of a white, feminist, heterosexual analysis of abuse, so Kanuha pointed out that acknowledging the abuse of lesbians of color could surely shatter some of the stability of the case against a white, male patriarchy.

Six years later, Waldron (1996) examined the impact of homophobia and racism on lesbians of color who are abused, lesbians of color who abuse, and lesbians of color who work within the movements to end woman abuse. She also offered suggestions for lesbians of color as communities.

Examination of the literature to date revealed that surveys and anecdotes have assumed the experience of white lesbians as normative. However, as Kanuha (1990a, 1990b) has pointed out, the original feminist analysis did not adequately include women of color, nor did the battered women's or sexual assault movements originally include issues facing women of color. If the movement to stop abuse in lesbian relationships is to avoid the same mistake, we must begin to attend to the unique barriers faced by women of color who have been abused and those who have abused.

If literature about lesbian abuse is scarce and literature about issues faced by lesbians of color scarcer still, the literature about lesbians who abuse is almost non-existent. One anonymous author contributed an article to Elliot's collection (1990), therapists circulated unpublished manuscripts about treatment for lesbians who abuse (e.g., Poorman & Gamache, 1985), and discussions took place at local, regional, and national conferences, but the topic had not been addressed openly in the literature. Eventually one author filled this void with a perspective about the individual pathology of lesbian abusers. Using her clinical experiences with abusers and a focused review of the literature to support her position, Coleman (1994) suggested that lesbian abusers have many of the characteristic personality features found among people with borderline and narcissistic personality disorders. Unlike male theorists who have broken with the feminist sociopolitical analyses of abuse to examine the role of individualized pathology (Dutton, 1998; Island & Letellier, 1992), Coleman clarified that understanding individual personality characteristics need not negate an understanding of the sociopolitical forces that undergird abuse. Rather, she suggested that understanding both individual and social forces may in combination enhance our overall understanding of abuse.

Descriptions of Approaches and Community Efforts

Approaches. Two studies have researched resources available to lesbians in abusive relationships with disturbing results. Wise and Bowman (1997) empirically examined therapist attitudes, approaches, and training related to abuse in lesbian relationships. Renzetti (1996) surveyed service providers to document their inclusion of lesbians in services that address abuse. Wise and Bowman (1997) found that counselors perceived heterosexual battering as more violent and were more likely to recommend charging a male batterer with assault than a female batterer. Further, while most therapists would not recommend couples counseling for heterosexual couples because of the issue of victim/survivor safety, most reported that they would recommend couples counseling for lesbians. Perhaps even more alarming was the finding that less than half of the masters- and doctoral-level counselors surveyed reported coursework or practical experience in dealing with domestic violence or lesbian concerns. When therapists reported coursework in either domestic abuse or lesbian issues, it was generally one class period and within one course.

It should not come as a surprise, then, that lesbians who have sought help from therapists stated that the therapists' approaches resulted in psychological or physical harm. Not "naming" the violence and directly or indirectly blaming the victim have been lesbians' primary concerns. Few hold the belief that both partners are being abusive in heterosexual relationships or that victim/survivor dependency explains why the abuse occurs. Nonetheless, fictions about mutual abuse and co-dependency have been resurrected to attempt to explain abuse in lesbian relationships. There is no research to support the belief that mutual abuse or co-dependency are more viable explanations of abuse in lesbian relationships than they are in heterosexual relationships (Asherah, 1990). They are considered variations of victim-blaming (Poorman, 1985; Poorman, Gilbert, & Simmons, 1990). Renzetti's research has highlighted the fact that therapy based on these beliefs is damaging to the victim/survivor of abuse in a lesbian relationship. Offering couples counseling has resulted in a documented lack of safety or in imminent harm (Renzetti, 1992). Battered lesbians have not only been victimized by their partners, but may be victimized again by those whose help they seek. Reports have documented that the overall experience of lesbian victims/survivors with service resources is that they are not accessible or perceived to be accessible. When services are accessed, they are often not helpful or may even be dangerous.

With the exception of Wise and Bowman (1997) and Renzetti (1996), other authors have based their comments about approaches to the problem of abuse in lesbian relationships on professional or clinical experiences. Margolies and Leeder (1995) offered some empirical description of the demographic characteristics of two groups of abusers ($N = 32$) seen for therapy and qualitatively described the therapy with these clients, including the therapists' reflections on the experiences. Istar (1996) discussed the merits of assessing couple dynamics. Hart (1986), Linda and Avreayl (1986), Leventhal (1990), Richards (1990), and Vecoli (1990) each discussed the needs of lesbian victims/survivors in terms of shelters, safe houses, and other safe spaces. Porat (1986) has described a support group for lesbian victims/survivors. Two articles have described and discussed guidelines specific to abuse in lesbian relationships for mental health providers (Poorman, Gilbert, & Simmons, 1990; Schecter, 1982).

Research has shown that when lesbians seek help from law enforcement, shelters, and safe homes/spaces, they do not perceive that help to be highly effective. Only 2% of abused lesbians surveyed have indicated that they would find intervention by police and courts helpful (Renzetti, 1992). Results of one study have shown that gay litigants are frequent targets of gratuitous homophobic asides from the benches of state and federal courts with criminal cases evidencing the most frequent asides. The longer the case, the more frequent the homophobic asides (Goldyn, 1981). Although nearly 20% of the lesbians surveyed stated that having a safe place to go would be helpful, they also cited the blatant homophobia of police, courts, and shelter staffs as their primary hesitation for not accessing these resources (Renzetti, 1992).

Causation theories. Service providers working in the mental health, criminal justice, and social service systems have addressed and described the needs of lesbian victims/survivors, but little has been written about the causes of lesbian relationship abuse. Some agreement exists that, irrespective of gender, it is the abuser who is responsible for the abuse and its effects. As the visibility of same-sex abuse has increased, abuser typologies focusing on individual demographics and pathology to the exclusion of social forces have begun to proliferate in the literature. A number of studies have attempted to collapse specific abuser personality traits into associated personality disorders, using measures like the Minnesota Multiphasic Personality Inventory (MMPI) or the Millon Clinical Multiaxial Inventory (MCMI; e.g., Caesar, 1988; Caesar & Hamberger, 1989; Hamberger & Hastings, 1986, 1988, 1991; Hastings & Hamberger, 1988). Findings have shown that when male batterers in treatment as a group were compared to non-batterers, the male batterers were more likely to exhibit characteristics of personality disorders, including schizoid, borderline, narcissistic, passive dependent and passive aggressive, and compulsive. While not empirically derived, Coleman's (1994) characterization of lesbian abusers also suggests an overrepresentation of borderline and narcissistic personality disorders among lesbian abusers seeking treatment.

These studies have identified important individual characteristics of pathology present in the clinical samples, and quantitative evidence has suggested that male abusers who fit these profiles do seem to constitute a larger proportion of the identified treatment population (Tolman & Bennet, 1990). However, as the studies themselves have reported, it would not be unlikely for clinical samples to include an overrepresentation of psychopathology among participants or to include more disturbed participants among the first to volunteer for or be mandated into treatment. Woman abuse is certainly not limited to those men (or women) with personality problems. Individual psychopathology is more easily measured than social pathology, but the presence of individual psychopathology does not negate social forces as a causal factor in abusive behavior. Further, even consistent overrepresentation of psychopathology does not implicate it as causal.

As with heterosexual and gay relationships, the sparse literature about abuse in lesbian relationships has offered theoretical perspectives about lesbian abuse focused either on individual abuser psychopathology or on social perspectives. Two articles have integrated psychological and social perspectives about the causes of lesbian abuse (Poorman, 1986; Poorman, Gilbert, & Simmons, 1990). The model presented in the articles outlined learning, opportunity, and decision as the three critical factors that must be present for abuse to occur. These factors were then linked directly to a group therapy model for abusers, a psychoeducational model for abused lesbians, and ecological interventions within communities. Extending this model in collaboration with the Violence in Lesbian Relationships (VLR) Task Force members, Zemsky (1990) integrated the impact of homophobia on each of the three causal factors. With these exceptions, few researchers have attempted to integrate a feminist sociopolitical analysis of abuse with the realities of lesbian abuse. While the models have been based on personal or clinical experience and informal qualitative study rather than quantitative evidence, they have offered a beginning point as well as a challenge to strict individualists.

Criminal justice system responses. While the literature in social sciences and social services is quite scarce, articles written about abuse in lesbian relationships in legal, law enforcement, or judicial journals have been even fewer. Several articles in law reviews have discussed attorney opinions about abuse in lesbian relationships. The most comprehensive of these has outlined causes, effects, and descriptions of the next necessary steps within the criminal justice system (Ristock, 1994). While a number of articles have addressed the role that perceptions and attributions about domestic abuse play in every step within the criminal justice system responses, with one recent exception (Poorman, Seelau, & Seelau, 2000), none have included perceptions of abuse in lesbian relationships. One study included gay men (Harris & Cook, 1994), and one attorney, mentioned earlier, traced her early district attorney office experiences and her concerns about the invisibility of abuse in lesbian relationships (West, 1992).

DISCUSSION

Planning effective intervention to address any social problem begins with identifying and defining the problem, the people affected by the problem, and the ways in which those people are affected. Epidemiological studies of prevalence and incidence data document how many people are affected by the problem and describe the characteristics of the problem. Theoretical perspectives outline causal factors and draw links to solutions. Descriptions and evaluation of approaches that have been used to intervene in the problem lead to the development of useful models and protocols and best practices to address the problem. Finally, prevention efforts address how to prevent the problem from occurring. Primary prevention seeks to impact the entire population before a problem exists and usually involves dissemination of information to the population as a whole. Secondary prevention targets those identified to be at greatest risk of developing the problem and includes them in activities thought to be essential to averting the problem or buffering them from its effects. Tertiary prevention addresses the needs of those already affected by a problem, in the hope of reducing the duration of the problem or the number of people affected.

Estimates of prevalence (e.g., Renzetti, 1992) have confirmed the problem and identified correlates of abuse in lesbian relationships. Studies of incidence characteristics have documented the form, frequency, and lethality of the abuse in lesbian relationships. Initial theorizing has suggested that homophobia plays a role in identifying abuse in lesbian relationships (Benowitz, 1986; Lobel, 1986; Zemsky, 1990). Preliminary studies have begun to systematically examine perceptions and attributions of same-sex abuse (Poorman, Seelau, & Seelau, 2000) and offer promise for mapping changes in criminal justice system responses.

Although anecdotal accounts of surviving abuse in lesbian relationships have chronicled the experiences of many courageous women, as yet there is no systematic, empirical study of the effects of abuse in lesbian relationships. There is reason to believe that although the abuse may take many of the same forms that men's abuse of women does, the effects of being abused by a woman may differ qualitatively. No research has documented these effects.

To date, although there has been a proliferation of research describing various abuser characteristics, there has been no systematic, empirical investigation of the characteristics of lesbians who abuse. Coleman's (1994) position that abusers are likely to demonstrate characteristics that resemble borderline or narcissistic personality disorders was based on clinical experience. Renzetti's (1992) correlational study about victim/survivor perceptions of abuse cannot be used to develop profiles of lesbian abusers. Studies directly assessing psychological characteristics of lesbian abusers could enhance therapeutic planning, particularly if linked to specific treatment objectives.

Whether through formal diversionary programs within the criminal justice system or informal self-referrals to therapy, many lesbians confronting abuse in a relationship have sought help from therapists. While some anecdotes and two studies have indicated that their experiences have been negative, more work remains. Little research has focused on the perceived effectiveness of these services and none has empirically evaluated the services being provided to lesbians who abuse or to those who have been abused.

Although perceived to be essential to planning strategies to prevent abuse in lesbian relationships, no research has documented risk and protective factors to determine whether some lesbians may be at greater risk for being abused or for abusing. It may be politically consistent with feminist analyses to suggest that *any* woman could be abused, but it may also be that those factors that increase risk of victimization have simply not been identified as yet. Neither have those factors been identified that may increase or mitigate the risk of some lesbians abusing. Identifying individual characteristics of lesbians who abuse may help in planning effective therapy. Identifying individual effects on lesbians who have been abused may help in providing protection and healing. But it is the identification of broader risk and protective factors that may facilitate more widespread prevention planning.

Models for therapy with male abusers now regularly recommend group work as a preferred therapeutic mechanism, and several researchers have advocated embedding group therapy in an ecological approach that addresses the social forces that influence battering (Edleson & Tolman, 1992; Hamberger, 1996; Hamberger & Hastings, 1991; Tolman & Bennett, 1990). One article has described a feminist ecological approach to therapy with lesbians who abuse that also suggests that group therapy is a preferred modality and that this should be but one facet of a multifaceted approach (Poorman, Gilbert, & Simmons, 1990). Models for group and individual therapy should be expanded to full descriptions and evaluations of the safety and effectiveness of therapies with abusers, support groups with victims/survivors, psychoeducational groups with victims/survivors, individual work, and perhaps as Istar (1996) suggests, even couples work. In addition to evaluating the safety and effectiveness of various therapeutic approaches or models for addressing abuse in lesbian relationships, training and consultation strategies and community outreach efforts should be fully described and evaluated for their effectiveness in order to assist other mental health professionals, advocates, trainers, consultants, and facilitators in planning effective topical interventions. Efficacy of different safety options for victims should be evaluated. Although many have opinions about whether battered women's shelters are actually prepared to offer safety to lesbian victims or whether the unique differences of lesbian victims necessitate safe home networks or alternate mechanisms for safety, these issues have not yet been empirically investigated.

Finally, while there is now important work documenting some of the correlates of abuse in lesbian relationships, there is much work needed to develop a comprehensive feminist understanding of what causes abuse that includes the reality of abuse in lesbian relationships. It is theories of causation that dictate direction for solutions. Although the fact of same-sex abuse has caused some to challenge and even break with feminist sociopolitical analyses of abuse, at least two articles suggest a social-psychological analysis that does not necessitate such a schism. Both suggest that abuse of women, whether by men or other women, is still the result of misogynist social learning, precipitated by the same opportunities created by misogynist social norms, traditions, mores, and a patriarchal criminal justice system, and is still implemented by the same individual decision-making process. Future theoretical analyses should include an examination of both the social and psychological forces that influence lesbians who abuse. Further, such theories should examine not only the psychological effects on victims/survivors, but the effects on later relationships, on lesbian and feminist communities, and on practitioners. Finally, any theoretical examination should include attention to the role homophobia plays in the causes, effects, and interventions. It is my position that fully understanding homophobia and heterosexism may be to understanding abuse in same-sex relationships what understanding sexism has been to understanding woman abuse by men. The dynamics of dominance and subordination appear to be at issue, regardless of the gender of victim and perpetrator.

What Are the Next Steps?

Anecdotal and empirical literature has amply documented that lesbians are also abused in relationships; that the abuse occurs with enough frequency not to be an anomaly; that it includes physical, sexual, emotional, and psychological abuse as well as threats; that it recurs and gets worse over time; and that it can be lethal. It is time to turn attention away from identifying that lesbians will also be clients and from the elusive tasks of documenting how many have been affected and characterizing and describing the incidents. The time has come to recognize and accept the fact that abuse continues to occur in lesbian relationships and that advocates, social service agencies, and mental health and criminal justice providers will continue to address and be forced to respond whether they have adequate information or not. It is my position that the most critical next steps will only be accomplished by forging links. Links must be forged between a number of groups who often hold only a piece of the puzzle and for whom mistrust of each other and territoriality has previously been the rule. Just as community intervention projects began to coordinate disparate community services for heterosexual abusers and victims/survivors (Gamache, Edleson, & Schock, 1988), I am suggesting that coordinated efforts, perhaps even formalized community intervention projects, involving law enforcement officers, attorneys, judges, mental health providers, advocates, social services personnel, and researchers may serve lesbians best. Further, coalitions that include those who have been active in movements to stop woman abuse by men could avoid reinventing the wheel. Efforts should be made to include lesbians of color in every phase of planning to avoid the disenfranchisement that the dominant battered women's movement and sexual assault movements have experienced.

The process of coalition building will probably be slower than any of us wishes. Service providers have long histories of mistrusting researchers, women of color long histories of mistrusting white women, and advocates long histories of mistrusting criminal justice and mental health professionals. Difficult as it may be, together, researchers, service providers, abused lesbians, and advocates can effectively take the next steps in ensuring safe, violence-free relationships for lesbians.

REFERENCES

Asherah, K. (1990). The myth of mutual abuse. In P. Elliot (Ed.), *Confronting lesbian battering* (pp. 56-58). St. Paul: Minnesota Coalition for Battered Women.

Barry, C. (1990). The importance of a name. In P. Elliot (Ed.), *Confronting lesbian battering* (pp. 127-131). St. Paul: Minnesota Coalition for Battered Women.

Benowitz, M. (1986). How homophobia affects lesbians' response to violence in lesbian relationships. In K. Lobel (Ed.), *Naming the violence: Speaking out about lesbian battering* (pp. 190-197). Seattle, WA: Seal.

Bologna, M. J., Waterman, C. K., & Dawson, L. J. (1987, July). *Violence in gay male and lesbian relationships: Implications for practitioners and policy makers.* Paper presented at 3rd National Conference for Family Violence Researchers, Durham, NH.

Bradford, J., Ryan, C., & Rothblum, E. D. (1994). National lesbian health care survey: Implications for mental health care. *Journal of Consulting and Clinical Psychology, 63,* 228-242.

Brand, P. A., & Kidd, A. H. (1986). Frequency of physical aggression in heterosexual and female homosexual dyads. *Psychological Reports, 59,* 1307-1313.

Caesar, P. L. (1988). Exposure to violence in the families of origin among wife abusers and maritally nonviolent men. *Violence and Victims, 3,* 49-63.

Caesar, P. L., & Hamberger, L. K. (1989). *Treating men who batter: Theory, practice, and programs.* New York: Springer.

Cardarelli, A. (Ed.). (1997). *Violence between intimate partners: Patterns, causes, and effects* (1st ed.). Needham Heights, MA: Allyn & Bacon.

Coleman, V. E. (1990). Violence between lesbian couples: A between-groups comparison. Unpublished doctoral dissertation. University Microfilms International No. 9109022.

Coleman, V. E. (1994). Lesbian battering: The relationship between personality and the perpetration of violence. *Violence and Victims, 9*(2), 139-152.

Crall, S. (1986). Love is not enough: An examination. In K. Lobel (Ed.), *Naming the violence: Speaking out about lesbian battering* (pp. 32-36). Seattle, WA: Seal.

Davies, D., & Neal, C. (1996). *Pink therapy: A guide for counsellors and therapists working with lesbian, gay, and bisexual clients.* Buckingham: Open University.

Duthu, K. F. (1996). Why doesn't anyone talk about gay and lesbian domestic violence? *Thomas Jefferson Law Review, 18,* 23-40.

Dutton, D. G. (1998). *The abusive personality: Violence and control in intimate relationships.* New York: Guilford.

Edgington, A. (1990). Anyone but me. In P. Elliot (Ed.), *Confronting lesbian battering* (pp. 120-126). St. Paul: Minnesota Coalition for Battered Women.

Edleson, J. L., & Tolman, R. M. (1992). *Intervention for men who batter: An ecological approach.* Newbury Park, CA: Sage.

Elliot, P. (1990). Shattering illusions: Same-sex domestic violence. *Journal of Gay & Lesbian Social Services, 4*(1), 1-8.

Faulkner, E. (1991). Lesbian abuse: The social and legal realities. *Queen's Law Journal, 16,* 261-286.

Gamache, D. J., Edleson, J. L., & Schock, M. D. (1988). Coordinated police, judicial and social service response to woman battering: A multi-baseline evaluation across three communities. In G. T. Hotalling, D. Finkelhor, J. T. Kilpatrick, & M. Straus (Eds.), *Responses to family violence: What we know and how to use it* (pp. 193-211). Newbury Park, CA: Sage.

Gardner, R. (1989). Method of conflict resolution and characteristics of abuse and victimization in heterosexual, lesbian, and gay male couples. Doctoral dissertation, University of Georgia. Dissertation Abstracts International, Vol. 50, 746B.

Goldfarb, P. (1996). Describing without circumscribing: Questioning the construction of gender in the discourse of intimate violence. *George Washington Law Review, 64*(3), 582-631.

Goldyn, L. (1981). Gratuitous language in appellate cases involving gay people: "Queer baiting" from the bench. *Political Behavior, 3*(1), 31-44.

Hamberger, L. K. (1996). Intervention in gay male intimate violence requires coordinated efforts on multiple levels. In C. M. Renzetti & C. H. Miley (Eds.), *Violence in gay and lesbian domestic partnerships* (pp. 83-91). Binghamton, NY: Harrington Park Press.

Hamberger, L. K., & Hastings, J. E. (1986). Personality correlates of men who abuse their partners: A cross validation study. *Journal of Family Violence, 1*, 323-341.

Hamberger, L. K., & Hastings, J. E. (1988). Characteristics of male spouse abusers consistent with personality disorders. *Hospital and Community Psychiatry, 39*(7), 763-770.

Hamberger, L. K., & Hastings, J. E. (1991). Personality correlates of men who batter and nonviolent men: Some continuities and discontinuities. *Journal of Family Violence, 6*, 131-147.

Harris, R. J., & Cook, C. A. (1994). Attributions about spouse abuse: It matters who the batterers and victims are. *Sex Roles, 30*, 553-565.

Hart, B. (1986). Lesbian battering: An examination. In K. Lobel (Ed.), *Naming the violence: Speaking out about lesbian battering* (pp. 173-189). Seattle, WA: Seal.

Hastings, J. E., & Hamberger, L. K. (1988). Personality characteristics of spouse abusers: A controlled comparison. *Violence and Victims, 3*(1), 31-47.

Hurley, K. (1986). Love as addiction. In K. Lobel (Ed.), *Naming the violence: Speaking out about lesbian battering* (pp. 56-61). Seattle, WA: Seal.

Island, D., & Letellier, P. (1992, July). *Battering disorders: Individual causation theory alternatives to heterosexist sociopolitical theory.* Paper presented at the annual meeting of the American Psychological Association, Washington, DC.

Istar, A. (1996). Couple assessment: Identifying and intervening in domestic violence in lesbian relationships. In C. M. Renzetti & C. H. Miley (Eds.), *Violence in gay and lesbian domestic partnerships* (pp. 93-106). New York: The Haworth Pess, Inc.

Kanuha, V. (1990a). Dealing with conflict in the battered women's movement. In P. Elliot (Ed.), *Confronting lesbian battering* (pp. 21-24). St. Paul: Minnesota Coalition for Battered Women.

Kanuha, V. (1990b). Compounding the triple jeopardy: Battering in lesbian of color relationships. *Women & Therapy, 9*, 169-184.

Kelly, E. E., & Warshafsky, L. (1987, July). *Partner abuse in gay male and lesbian couples.* Paper presented at the Third National Conference for Family Violence Researchers, Durham, NH.

Leeder, E. (1988). Enmeshed in pain: Counseling the lesbian battering couple. *Women & Therapy, 7*, 81-99.

Leventhal, B. (1990). Confronting lesbian battering. In P. Elliot (Ed.), *Confronting lesbian battering* (pp. 16-18). St. Paul: Minnesota Coalition for Battered Women.

Lie, G. Y., & Gentlewarrior, S. (1991). Intimate violence in lesbian relationships: Discussion of survey findings and practice implications. *Journal of Social Service Research, 15*, 41-59.

Lie, G. W., Schilit, R., Bush, J., Montagne, M., & Reyes, L. (1991). Lesbians in currently aggressive relationships: How frequently do they report aggressive past relationships. *Violence and Victims, 6*, 121-135.

Linda, & Avreayl. (1986). Organizing safe space for battered lesbians: A community based program. In K. Lobel (Ed.), *Naming the violence: Speaking out about lesbian battering* (pp. 103-110). Seattle, WA: Seal.

Lisa (1986). Once hitting starts. In K. Lobel (Ed.), *Naming the violence: Speaking out about lesbian battering* (pp. 37-40). Seattle, WA: Seal.

Lobel, K. (Ed.). (1986). *Naming the violence: Speaking out about lesbian battering.* Seattle, WA: Seal.

Lockhart, L., White, B. A., Causby, V., & Isaac, A. (1994). Letting out the secret: Violence in lesbian relationships. *Journal of Interpersonal Violence, 9*(4), 469-493.

Loulan, J. (1987). *Lesbian passion: Loving ourselves and each other.* San Francisco: Spinsters/Aunt Lute.

Lupton, C., & Gillespie, T. (1994). *Working with violence.* Hampshire: McMillan.

Margolies, L., & Leeder, E. (1995). Violence at the door: Treatment of lesbian batterers. *Violence Against Women, 1*(2), 139-157.

Marie, S. (1984). [Letter in Open Forum]. *Victimology: An International Journal,* 17-20.

Martin, D. (1981). *Battered wives.* San Francisco: Volcano.

National Coalition of Anti-Violence Programs. (1998). *Annual report on lesbian, gay, bisexual, transgender domestic violence.* Washington DC: Author.

Northwood, B. (1986). She never really hit me. In K. Lobel (Ed.), *Naming the violence: Speaking out about lesbian battering* (pp. 148-154). Seattle, WA: Seal.

Pagelow, M. (1984). *Family violence.* New York: Praeger.

Poorman, P. B. (1985). Causes and fictions about violence against women. Unpublished manuscript.

Poorman, P. B. (1986). Definitions of abuse. Unpublished manuscript.

Poorman, P. B., & Gamache, D. (1985). Working with lesbians who abuse their partners: A description of a group intervention model. Unpublished manuscript.

Poorman, P. B., Gilbert, L., & Simmons, S. L. (1990). Guidelines for mental health systems response to lesbian battering. In P. Elliot (Ed.), *Confronting lesbian battering* (pp. 105-118). St. Paul: Minnesota Coalition for Battered Women.

Poorman, P. B., & Seelau, S. M. (2001). Lesbians who abuse their partners: Using the FIRO-B to assess interpersonal characteristics. *Women & Therapy.*

Poorman, P. B., Seelau, E. P., & Seelau, S. M. (2000). *Perceptions of domestic abuse in same-sex relationships and implications for criminal justice and mental health responses.* Manuscript submitted for publication.

Porat, N. (1986). Support groups for battered lesbians. In K. Lobel (Ed.), *Naming the violence: Speaking out about lesbian battering* (pp. 80-87). Seattle, WA: Seal.

Renzetti, C. M. (1988). Violence in lesbian relationships: A preliminary analysis of causal factors. *Journal of Interpersonal Violence, 3,* 381-399.

Renzetti, C. M. (1989). Building a second closet: Third-party responses to victims of lesbian partner abuse. *Family Relations, 38,* 157-163.

Renzetti, C. M. (1992). *Violent betrayal: Partner abuse in lesbian relationships* (1st ed.). Newbury Park, CA: Sage.

Renzetti, C. M. (1996). The poverty of services for battered lesbians. In C. M. Renzetti & C. H. Miley (Eds.), *Violence in gay and lesbian domestic partnerships* (pp. 61-68). Binghamton, NY: Harrington Park Press.

Renzetti, C. M. (1997). Violence and abuse among same-sex couples. In A. Cardarelli (Ed.), *Violence between intimate partners: Patterns, causes, and effects* (1st ed., pp. 70-89). Needham Heights, MA: Allyn & Bacon.

Richards, L. (1990). Advocacy for lesbians in abusive relationships. In P. Elliot (Ed.), *Confronting lesbian battering* (pp. 93-99). St. Paul: Minnesota Coalition for Battered Women.

Ristock, J. L. (1994). "And justice for all?" . . . The social context of legal responses to abuse in lesbian relationships. *Canadian Journal of Women in Law, 7,* 415-430.

Schecter, S. (1982). *Women and male violence: The visions and struggles of the battered women's movement.* Boston: South End.

Schilit, R., Lie, G., & Montagne, M. (1990). Substance use as a correlate of violence in intimate, lesbian relationships. *Journal of Homosexuality, 19,* 51-65.

Sherrod, D., & Nardi, P. (1998). Homophobia in the courtroom: An assessment of biases against gay men and lesbians in a multiethnic sample. In G. Herek (Ed.), *Stigma and sexual orientation: Understanding prejudice against lesbians, gay men, and bisexuals* (1st ed., pp. 24-38). Thousand Oaks, CA: Sage.

Singer, B. L., & Deschamps, D. (Eds.). (1994). *Gay and lesbian stats.* New York: New York Press.

Sloan, L., & Edmond, T. (1996). Shifting the focus: Recognizing the needs of lesbian and gay survivors of sexual violence. *Journal of Gay & Lesbian Social Services, 5*(4), 33-51.

Steinem, G. (1983). Keynote address presented at the National Coalition Against Sexual Assault Conference, Minneapolis, MN.

Straus, M. A. (1979). Measuring intrafamily conflict and violence: The Conflict Tactics (CT) Scales. *Journal of Marriage and the Family, 41,* 75-88.

Straus, M. A. (1989). The Conflict Tactics Scales and its' critics: An evaluation of new data on validity and reliability. In M. A. Straus & R. J. Gelles (Eds.), *Physical violence in American families* (pp. 49-74). New Brunswick, NJ: Transaction.

Tolman, R. M., & Bennett, L. M. (1990). A review of quantitative research on men who batter. *Journal of Interpersonal Violence, 5*(1), 87-118.

Vecoli, L. (1990). The shelter's response to lesbian battering. In P. Elliot (Ed.), *Confronting lesbian battering* (pp. 73-74). St. Paul: Minnesota Coalition for Battered Women.

Waldner-Haugrud, L., & Gratch, L. (1997). Sexual coercion in gay/lesbian relationships: Descriptives and gender differences. *Violence and Victims, 12,* 87-96.

Waldner-Haugrud, L., Gratch, L., & Magruder, B. (1997). Victimization and perpetration rates of violence in gay and lesbian relationships: Gender issues explored. *Violence and Victims, 12,* 173-182.

Waldron, C. M. (1996). Lesbians of color and the domestic violence movement. In C. M. Renzetti & C. H. Miley (Eds.), *Violence in gay and lesbian domestic partnerships* (pp. 42-51). Binghamton, NY: Harrington Park Press.

Waterman, C. K., Dawson, L. J., & Bologna, M. J. (1989). Sexual coercion in gay male and lesbian relationships: Predictors and implications for support services. *Journal of Sex Research, 26,* 118-124.

West, A. (1992). Prosecutorial activism: Confronting heterosexism in a lesbian battering case. *Harvard Women's Law Journal, 15,* 249-271.

Wise, A., & Bowman, S. (1997). Comparison of beginning counselors' responses to lesbian vs. heterosexual partner abuse. *Violence and Victims, 12,* 127-134.

Zemsky, B. (1990). Lesbian battering: Considerations for intervention. In P. Elliot (Ed.), *Confronting lesbian battering* (pp. 64-67). St. Paul: Minnesota Coalition for Battered Women.

Nowhere to Hide:
Lesbian Battering, Homophobia, and Minority Stress

Kimberly F. Balsam

SUMMARY. This article examines the relationship between lesbian battering, homophobia (both external and internalized), and the stress of living as a member of an oppressed minority. While domestic violence in lesbian relationships parallels domestic violence in heterosexual relationships in many ways, the context of homophobia in society, in addition to sexism, creates some unique dynamics, issues, and barriers to change. Drawing upon a review of the theoretical and empirical literature, as well as the author's clinical experience as a lesbian psychotherapist, the impact of the homophobic context on lesbian battering is examined from the perspective of victims, perpetrators, and helping systems. *[Article copies available for a fee from The Haworth Document Delivery Service: 1-800-342-9678. E-mail address: <getinfo@haworthpressinc.com> Website: <http://www.HaworthPress.com> © 2001 by The Haworth Press, Inc. All rights reserved.]*

KEYWORDS. Lesbian battering, lesbians, domestic violence, homophobia, internalized homophobia, minority stress

---

Kimberly F. Balsam, MS, is a doctoral student in the clinical psychology program at the University of Vermont. Her clinical, research and teaching interests focus on the psychology of women and lesbian, gay, and bisexual psychology.

Address correspondence to: Kimberly F. Balsam, Department of Psychology, John Dewey Hall, University of Vermont, Burlington, VT 05405 (E-mail: Kimfern@aol.com).

[Haworth co-indexing entry note]: "Nowhere to Hide: Lesbian Battering, Homophobia, and Minority Stress." Balsam, Kimberly F. Co-published simultaneously in *Women & Therapy* (The Haworth Press, Inc.) Vol. 23, No. 3, 2001, pp. 25-37; and: *Intimate Betrayal: Domestic Violence in Lesbian Relationships* (ed: Ellyn Kaschak) The Haworth Press, Inc., 2001, pp. 25-37. Single or multiple copies of this article are available for a fee from The Haworth Document Delivery Service [1-800-342-9678, 9:00 a.m. - 5:00 p.m. (EST). E-mail address: getinfo@haworthpressinc.com].

Lesbian battering exists. This much we know. Public awareness of domestic violence in lesbian relationships has come gradually, painstakingly, and with reservations by many. The beginnings of the battered women's movement in the 1970s emphasized male violence against women, leaving little room for explaining relationships in which women were perpetrators of violence. The Lesbian Task Force of the National Coalition Against Domestic Violence was the first group to address publicly lesbian battering in 1983. Shortly afterwards, the first book on the topic, *Naming the Violence: Speaking Out About Lesbian Battering,* appeared, providing a voice for survivors and activists and beginning the process of educating the lesbian community and the battered women's movement about this issue. In this book, Hart (1986) provided a definition of lesbian battering that has often been cited:

> Lesbian battering is a pattern of violent or coercive behaviors whereby a lesbian seeks to control the thoughts, beliefs, or conduct of her intimate partner or to punish the intimate for resisting the perpetrator's control. Individual acts of physical violence, by this definition, do not constitute lesbian battering. Physical violence is not battering unless it results in the enhanced control of the batterer over the recipient. (p. 173)

As more women began to speak out about their experiences of domestic violence in lesbian relationships, empirical researchers in the social sciences began to investigate prevalence rates. Research to date has yielded a wide range of estimates ranging from 7% to 48% for physical abuse, and up to 90% when verbal abuse is included (see Burke & Follingstad, 1999, for a review). These figures must be approached with caution, as the existing body of research is hampered by a number of methodological weaknesses. Some of these issues are the same as those faced by other lesbian/gay/bisexual researchers, such as recruitment of representative samples, small sample sizes, homogeneous (well-educated, White, middle-class) samples, etc. Some studies have failed to assess the gender of the perpetrator, and, therefore, fail to separate abuse by previous male partners and abuse by female partners. Furthermore, the range of operational definitions and measures makes comparisons between studies of lesbian battering and comparisons with studies of heterosexual battering difficult (Burke & Follingstad, 1999). Nevertheless, research to date suggests that lesbian battering occurs with a frequency that is alarming. It is no longer possible to ignore this serious social problem.

Unfortunately, the response of the lesbian community and the battered women's movement has, to date, been less than adequate. For example, Renzetti (1988), in a sample of 100 battered lesbians, found that "few respondents sought help from hotlines and women's shelters, and of those who did, most found them to be no help at all or only a little helpful. Other institutional sources of help, such as the police, attorneys, physicians, and psychiatrists, proved to be the least helpful of all . . . In total, 64% (of the respondents) stayed (in the abusive relationship) because they 'did not know where, or how, to seek help' " (p. 395). In a later study, Renzetti (1995) reported that out of 566 domestic violence service agencies surveyed, only 9.3% offered services targeted to meet the needs of battered lesbians. Perhaps of more concern is the finding that "The majority reported that they had no plans to expand their services for battered lesbians" (p. 123).

What factors might contribute to the lack of response? Focusing on prevalence rates may obscure the fact that domestic violence in lesbian relationships differs from domestic violence in heterosexual relationships in a number of important ways. Most importantly, lesbian battering occurs in a context of homophobia. Pharr (1986) explained succinctly:

> There is an important difference between the battered lesbian and the battered non-lesbian: the battered non-lesbian experiences violence within the context of a misogynist world; the lesbian experiences violence within the context of a world that is not only woman-hating, but is also homophobic. (p. 204)

Without careful attention to context, we cannot begin to understand the unique factors that have kept lesbian battering hidden, and, more recently, have inhibited adequate response. A closer examination of the complex and multifaceted ways that homophobia influences the experience of lesbian battering might help us to understand this lack of response and point to more effective future interventions.

The purpose of this article is to explore the impact of homophobia and minority stress in the lives of lesbians and to examine ways that it might impact the experience of lesbian battering for the victim, the perpetrator, and sources of help.

HOMOPHOBIA

Weinberg (1972) coined the term "homophobia" to describe the irrational fear, hatred and intolerance of homosexuality. This definition places homophobia in parallel with other irrational "phobias." Contemporary activists and theorists, however, tend to view homophobia as linked with sexism, racism, classism, and other "isms"–forms of oppression of one group of people by another group based on a particular characteristic or trait, rather than a clinical "phobia." Consequently, some have proposed that "heterosexism" is a more appropriate term. Herek (1990) defines this term as "an ideological system that denies, denigrates, and stigmatizes any non-heterosexual form of behavior, identity, relationship, and community" (p. 316). For the purposes of this paper, the words will be used interchangeably.

The homophobic context means that intimate lesbian lives and lesbian relationships are pathologized by the dominant culture. Milestones in family development such as dating, marriage, pregnancy, child-rearing, retirement, and illness are all shaped and restricted by lack of role models, social approval, and legal and institutional support. When progress is made toward legitimating lesbian relationships, backlash usually follows, bringing homophobic stereotypes and prejudice even more out in the open. The recent passing of the Civil Union legislation in Vermont, followed by the rise of anti-LGB sentiment and political action throughout the state, is a very tangible reminder of this.

The feminist response to domestic violence has included the awareness that it occurs in a context of violence against women in society. Women's vulnerability extends beyond their risk in the home. Whether or not a woman has previously been a victim of other male violence, she is invariably aware of the threat of such violence. This awareness shapes her experience of violence within the home. Similarly, lesbian battering takes place against a backdrop of violence against women and homophobic violence against gays, lesbians and bisexuals. Berrill (1992), in a review of 24 studies, found that 80% of lesbians, gays, and bisexuals report having experienced verbal harassment, 44% report threats of violence, 33% report being chased or followed, 17% report being physically assaulted. In a more recent study of 2000 lesbian, gay, and bisexual adults, 20% of women and 25% of men reported experiencing victimization based on their sexual orientation (Herek, Gillis, & Cogan, 1999). Such victimization has an even greater impact on mental health and well-being than non-bias related attacks.

In a broader sense, we can see homophobia and violence as inevitably interconnected. Neisen (1993) refers to heterosexism as a form of "cultural victimization" that parallels other victimizations such as rape and abuse in its impact on individuals' well-being. Almeida, Woods, Messineo, Font, and Heer (1994) describe a "hierarchy" of oppression. In this hierarchy, white heterosexual men are at the top of the power structure, then white heterosexual women, white gay men and lesbians, heterosexual men and women of color, and lesbians and gay men of color. We might also add groups such as immigrants, disabled people, old people, and others who differ from "the norm" to the lower rungs of this hierarchy. If power and privilege accompany higher status in the hierarchy of oppression, we can see violence, in all its manifestations, as a tool that enforces the hierarchy.

Internalized Homophobia

Internalized homophobia has been defined as the internalization by lesbians, gay men, and bisexuals of negative attitudes and assumptions about homosexuality (Shidlo, 1994; Sophie, 1987). In models of sexual identity development, it is seen as being most acute early in the coming out process, as an individual struggles to reconcile his or her own private feelings with the stigmatized view of homosexuality in the outside world (Cass, 1984; Coleman, 1982). In its most overt form, it manifests as a hatred of one's homosexuality, the belief that one is "sick" for being LGB, and the desire to change one's sexuality. However, internalized homophobia can persist even after the initial stages of the coming out process, and even if the individual appears outwardly to have come to terms with his or her sexual orientation. In more covert forms, it can manifest as a discomfort with other LGB people, attempting to "pass" as heterosexual, and feelings of shame and guilt about one's sexual orientation. Negative feelings, attitudes and beliefs about self and other lesbians, gays, and bisexuals can become integrated into an individual's identity, and are inevitably reinforced by messages from society. Not surprisingly, internalized homophobia in lesbians has been empirically linked with lower social support, lack of connection with the lesbian community, loneliness, low self-esteem, and depression (Szymanski & Chung, in press; Szymanski, Chung, & Balsam, in press).

Minority Stress

One approach to conceptualizing the impact of homophobia on the individual lesbian, gay, or bisexual person is the notion of "minority stress." Brooks (1981) provides a useful explanation:

> The initial cause of minority stress is the cultural ascription of inferior status to particular groups. This ascription of defectiveness to various categories of people, particularly categories based on sex, race, and sociosexual preference, often precipitates negative life events for the minority member over which the individual has little control. (p. 71)

Brooks pointed out that lesbians are doubly at risk for such "negative life events" given their multiple minority status as women and lesbians. For lesbians of color, lesbians in poverty, lesbians with disabilities, lesbians who are immigrants, and others who are members of marginalized groups, the risk multiplies even further.

DiPlacido (1998) provides a broader model of minority stress in the lives of lesbians, gays, and bisexuals. She makes the distinction between internal stressors and external stressors. Internalized homophobia is seen as an internal stressor, arising from within the individual, and presenting "a major roadblock to well-being for many lesbians, gay men, and bisexuals" (p. 147). Self-concealment and emotional inhibition are hypothesized to be additional internal stressors. While being completely or partially closeted may serve as a buffer against some overt forms of homophobic discrimination and violence, the stress of "hiding" may have particularly deleterious effects on well-being. Indeed, Morris (1997) found a strong correlation between degree of "outness" and mental well-being in a large, diverse sample of lesbians.

DiPlacido's (1998) model of minority stress also examines external stressors including anti-LGB violence, anti-LGB discrimination, and daily hassles. She cites the general literature on stress, which tends to conceptualize stress in terms of life events and daily hassles, both of which have been linked empirically to health and mental health outcomes. Although little research examines the impact of stress on lesbians, DiPlacido hypothesizes that the experience and threat of anti-LGB violence and discrimination (e.g., loss of custody of children, lower wages than same-sex counterparts at work, restricted access to housing) put lesbians at great risk for "negative life events." Furthermore, she cites daily hassles such as "hearing antigay jokes" and "always being on guard" as more chronic stressors experienced by lesbians.

While much of DiPlacido's model awaits empirical investigation in lesbian samples, it is useful as an integrated explanation of the multifaceted ways that the context of homophobia impacts the lives of lesbians. The rest of this paper will begin to explore some of the specific ways that this context is significant in understanding the phenomenon of lesbian battering.

Context of Homophobia: Impact on Victim

Laura, a 41-year-old Caucasian lesbian, presents for therapy to deal with depression and anxiety. In therapy, she begins to relate these symptoms to the aftermath of a violent rape that occurred by her stepbrother when she was 12. She admits after five months of therapy that her partner of seven years "pushes me around sometimes." In fact, this past weekend during the heat of an argument, she grabbed Laura's arms and slammed her up against a wall, leaving several bruise marks on her arms. Laura downplays the significance of this to her therapist, stating that "I really provoked her this time, I should know better." Laura explains that she would never tell her family, who lives nearby, about the violence. "When I told them about being gay they couldn't accept it. Now Eileen is in my life, and at least my mom has finally come around. How could I give her a reason to reject me again?" Laura becomes tearful as she explains "I'm all Eileen has in this world. I would never do anything to make people think badly of her."

Homophobia and minority stress may impact on the victim in several ways. Using Neisen's (1993) concept of "cultural victimization," we can see the potential for interaction between the trauma-related feelings of guilt, shame, depression, and lack of self-worth resulting from both the homophobic context and the experience of domestic violence. She may blame herself for the abuse, or see it as a natural consequence of choosing a lesbian lifestyle. Neisen (1993) draws parallels between the self-blame that often occurs in victims of sexual and physical victimization ("I deserve to be abused; it's all my fault") and the self-blame that may occur because of being a lesbian ("Maybe gay people are sick and I deserve to be put down, beat up, etc."). These internalized homophobic messages may interact with more overt messages she receives from her abuser.

It is also important to take into account the concept of re-victimization in understanding the traumatic impact of lesbian battering on the victim. Empirical research has repeatedly demonstrated that individuals who experience traumatic victimization are at greater risk of other victimization experiences in the future (e.g., Banyard, Arnold, & Smith, 2000; Messman & Long, 1996). Furthermore, there appears to be a cumulative effect of trauma, such that re-victimization experiences lead to even worse mental health outcomes and more difficulty coping with trauma. The statistics on anti-LGB violence and harassment indicate that the victim of lesbian battering has most likely experienced at least some form of verbal, physical or sexual victimization. Furthermore, she may have been the victim of verbal, physical, or sexual violence in her family of origin as a result of her perceived sexual orientation and/or gender-role orientation. The multiple layers of victimization in the lives of many battered lesbians compound the experience of trauma and its impact on mental health and well-being.

Finally, asking for help may be severely impacted by homophobia. Feminist models of domestic violence in heterosexual relationships have illuminated the many barriers, both internal and external, that prevent women from leaving their abusive partners. While these barriers may apply to battered lesbians as well, other factors related to the homophobic context might come into play. Neisen (1993) makes the point that while victims of domestic violence can leave the abusive environment as part of their healing process, lesbians cannot leave a homophobic society and culture. To reach out for help involves a degree of trust, and a lesbian may be particularly reluctant to make herself vulnerable to others, and may fear subtle or overt homophobic reactions from help providers.

If the victim is partially or completely closeted, this poses additional factors that may impact her experience. If she is not connected with a lesbian community, she may not know other lesbians and may feel that leaving her partner would mean being single and isolated. Her partner may have threatened to "out" her to family, friends, coworkers, or other members of their community. In addition to the psychological and social implications of this threat, there is the very real threat that this "outing" would expose her to even greater danger of hate crimes. Less overt messages, such as "It's okay to be gay, but not to talk about it" may also have been internalized, making her reluctant to "rock the boat" by drawing attention to her lesbian relationship.

If the victim is "out" and involved with the lesbian community, she may feel that she has an image to uphold. If she is in a long-term relationship, she may receive the message from her community that she is a role model, and may fear loss of support if she damages this public image. She may also see herself as a model for the heterosexuals in her life, and may fear that her experience will lead others to judge all lesbians negatively, confirming negative homophobic stereotypes, if she reveals the violence. Her sense of loyalty to her batterer may be impacted by homophobia. She may see the impact of homophobic violence, discrimination, or hassles on her partner, and empathize with this pain.

Context of Homophobia: Impact on Perpetrator

Mary, a 28-year-old Latina lesbian, is referred to therapy by her girlfriend for "anger management." Mary admits to "slapping her girlfriend around" when she "gets too mouthy." She acknowledges that this is hurtful to the relationship, but wonders "what else would I do? I'm up to here with stress already, I can't take it when she goes off on me like that." She states that she witnessed her father beating her mother on a regular basis when she was growing up. After her father left her mother for another woman, her mother dated a series of violent men. Mary says she made the decision early on "that I wasn't ever gonna be some man's punching bag." In fact, she says that she sometimes disrespects her girlfriend for staying with her after "I get physical with her." On several occasions, when men in her neighborhood have made homophobic remarks, she threatened or physically attacked them. One of these confrontations led to Mary being beaten severely, leaving her with chronic pain and nerve damage in her left arm.

The feminist literature on battering in heterosexual relationships emphasizes battering as a tool to maintain power and control. In heterosexual couples, this means that the man enforces his male privilege through the use of violence. However, the issues of power and privilege and their impact on battering must be examined more closely in dealing with couples who differ from the white, heterosexual norm (Almeida et al., 1994). Lesbian batterers are multiply disempowered as women and as lesbians. Battering of a female partner, then, is not so clearly an enforcement of the social hierarchy, but a complex expression of multiple social and personal factors.

When a lesbian couple differs in terms of race, class, disability, or immigration status, issues of power and privilege can play out in a number of ways. The partner whose status is more "privileged" may exert this privilege in subtle ways, leading the less "privileged" partner to attempt to establish power and control through violence. Almeida et al. (1994) explain: "Within an interracial couple, the partner who can 'pass' for white usually accrues more social power through his or her affiliation with the privileged majority. This often influences intimate relationships by mirroring the imbalance of power created in the societal context . . . " (p. 119). Alternatively, the partner with more privilege may attempt to use this privilege to control and abuse her partner.

Living with the very real stresses of homophobia may fuel the violence. A batterer may experience herself as a victim in the outside world. She may encounter verbal or physical homophobic attacks, discrimination at work, or rejection from family and friends. Her intimate relationship may provide a context in which she feels the need to assume a position of power and control, taking herself out of the "victim" role. Alternatively, she may view her partner's actions as "provoking" the violence, and therefore view herself as a victim in her relationship as well. For the lesbian who has been the victim of male-induced violence, using violence as a strategy may signify resistance to the cultural stereotype of woman as victim. Violence as a strategy may appear to be the only acceptable alternative to this stereotype.

Homophobia, both external and internalized, may translate into lack of a social support network. The batterer may be cut off from family of origin or other possible sources of support. Negative feelings about homosexuality may impact her ability to make meaningful connections with the lesbian/gay/bisexual community. This isolation can create a sense of dependency on the partner. Renzetti (1992) found that the batterer's dependency on her partner, rather than the victim's dependency, was a risk factor for more severe and more frequent violence. This was especially true if the victim exerted the desire to be more independent. Institutional homophobia prevents lesbians from gaining legal ties, which may create a sense of relationships being unstable. Renzetti (1992) also found jealousy to be a strong correlate of battering behaviors.

Context of Homophobia: Impact on Sources of Help

In the early 1990s I was employed in a feminist/lesbian bookstore. The store served as an information and resource center for the local women's community, with bulletin boards and notebooks full of information. One morning, during my shift, a member of the newly formed local lesbian battering task force came into the store. She requested permission to leave a stack of pamphlets with basic information about lesbian battering in the resource room. I consented. Later that day, the store manager found them. She appeared hurt and angry, exclaiming "how could they leave something like that here!" The message, loud and clear, was that making this issue visible would portray lesbians in a negative light.

In oppressive environments, an "us/them" mentality can become a way of survival for the oppressed group. The lack of support, affirmation, and recognition of lesbians by the larger culture creates an intense need for a community in which lesbianism is affirmed. The prevalence of sexist and homophobic violence leaves many in the lesbian community longing for a "safe space" where these threats do not exist. Recognition of lesbian battering, violence perpetrated by and against our own, shatters this sense of safety. The reality of homophobia gives lesbians important reasons to protect our image, both inside and outside of the community. Almeida et al. (1994) explain: "Domestic violence enacted in response to public violence often is used as evidence by the dominant culture to support notions of the 'other's' inherent inferiority." Furthermore, the minority stress experienced by lesbians, especially those who are active in social change movements, may create a sense of "burnout" and reluctance to take on another complex social issue.

In the battered women's movement, a similar "us/them" mentality is often drawn along gender lines. Women are seen as victims, men as batterers. Men who batter are often viewed as incapable of change, and are excluded from systems working for change. Criminal prosecution is often seen as the most appropriate treatment for batterers. At the very least, treatment of batterers is generally conducted separately from treatment of victims in order to ensure safety for everyone. The lesbian community may be reluctant to recognize fully the danger that lesbian battering represents because to do so would raise questions about drawing similar lines within our own community. In a society that already denigrates and excludes lesbians, it may be difficult to consider ostracizing our own. Furthermore, much of the work of the lesbian/gay/bisexual rights movement over the past three decades has been to de-pathologize individual lesbians, gays, and bisexuals and shift responsibility for our distress back onto the shoulders of society. An acknowledgement that some lesbians abuse their partners raises difficult questions about the relative roles of individual responsibility and the impact of oppressive social forces on such behavior.

Who is worthy to be defined as a victim? All too often, helping systems respond to complex social problems by organizing experience into categories of "good" and "bad." While this rigid thinking style may be a response to the stresses of dealing with difficult issues, it can seriously impede the ability to understand and help those whose lives are outside of the "norm." For example, Renzetti (1999) points out that "femininity" has often been equated with "victim status":

> I found, when conducting my research on lesbian battering, that many heterosexuals were not at all surprised by the abuse itself. After all, they said, lesbians really want to be men, and men are often violent. Not surprisingly, then, many struggled with applying the label "victim" to the abused partner, since lesbians, by this definition, were masculine and could successfully repel an attacker. Consequently, lesbian abuse victims who had a masculine appearance, whose abusers appeared more feminine, and who did fight back faced tremendous obstacles when they sought help. (p. 48-49)

Heterosexist assumptions about gender roles and gender expression can therefore lead to victim-blaming and invisibility for lesbians who are battered.

In the battered women's movement, homophobia further impacts the availability of appropriate response. Suzanne Pharr (1988) made the argument that homophobia serves as a weapon of sexism. As long as women are afraid that to be labeled "feminist" is akin to being labeled "lesbian," an even more stigmatized role, they are less likely to become involved in feminist activities and thus the status quo is not threatened. This dynamic can be seen in the battered women's movement as well. Fear among heterosexual shelter workers and activists of being identified as "lesbian" may lead to tensions with staff who are lesbian or bisexual, and reluctance to address the issue of lesbian battering.

The specific setting in which help is provided to victims of domestic violence must also be examined. The battered women's movement has given rise to a network of shelters and safe homes across the U.S. These agencies are often the first line of intervention for women who are leaving domestically violent relationships. Most shelters have "women only" policies. For heterosexual women coming to these shelters, as well as shelter staff, it may be the first time that they are in such an environment. Some battered women may have been isolated from other women by their batterer, others may have been accused of lesbianism by their batterers in an attempt to control their contact with female friends. Battered heterosexual women may hold homophobic views and may feel uncomfortable living in the shelter with lesbians. Thus, while social service organizations as a whole may be impacted by homophobia, the setting of the domestic violence shelter creates unique challenges.

CONCLUSIONS AND SUGGESTIONS FOR FUTURE RESEARCH

Over the past two decades, survivors, activists, researchers and scholars have brought lesbian battering into the public eye. Much work remains, however, in understanding the factors unique to lesbian battering. Feminist theory and interventions addressing domestic violence have illuminated the relationship between domestic violence as a private experience and sexism as a societal experience. In order to begin to understand lesbian battering, we must examine more closely and thoroughly the impact of the sociocultural context on the ways that lesbian battering manifests and is experienced by victims, perpetrators, the lesbian community and helping systems. While we have done much to bring lesbian battering out of hiding, we must also acknowledge that for the battered lesbian, there is nowhere to hide from the pervasive and devastating effects of homophobia. It is incumbent upon researchers, theorists, and activists to continue to work towards developing models to understand and address lesbian battering that adequately take this into account.

REFERENCES

Almeida, R., Woods, R., Messineo, T., Font, R., & Heer, C. (1994). Violence in the lives of the racially and sexually different: A public and private dilemma. *Journal of Feminist Family Therapy, 5(3/4)*, 99-126.

Banyard, V. L., Arnold, S., & Smith, J. (2000). Childhood sexual abuse and dating experiences of undergraduate women. *Child Maltreatment, 5(1)*, 39-48.

Berrill, K. T. (1992). Anti-gay violence and victimization in the United States: An overview. In G. M. Herek & K. T. Berrill (Eds.), *Hate crimes: Confronting violence against lesbians and gay men.*

Brooks, V. R. (1981). *Minority stress and lesbian women.* Lexington, MA: Lexington Books.

Burke, L. K., & Follingstad, D. R. (1999). Violence in lesbian and gay relationships: Theory, prevalence, and correlational factors. *Clinical Psychology Review, 19(5)*, 487-512.

Cass, V. C. (1984). Homosexual identity formation: Testing a theoretical model. *Journal of Sex Research, 20*, 143-167.

Coleman, E. (1982). Developmental stages of the coming out process. *Journal of Homosexuality, 7(2-3)*, 31-43.

DiPlacido, J. (1998). Minority stress among lesbians, gay men, and bisexuals: A consequence of heterosexism, homophobia, and stigmatization. In G. M. Herek (Ed.), *Stigma and sexual orientation: Understanding prejudice against lesbians, gay men, and bisexuals* (pp. 138-159). Thousand Oaks, CA: Sage.

Hart, B. (1986). Lesbian battering: An examination. In K. Lobel (Ed.), *Naming the violence* (pp. 173-189). Seattle: Seal Press.

Herek, G. M. (1990). The context of anti-gay violence: Notes on cultural and psychological heterosexism. *Journal of Interpersonal Violence, 5*, 316-333.

Herek, G. M., Gillis, J. R., & Cogan, J. C. (1999). Psychological sequelae of hate-crime victimization among lesbian, gay, and bisexual adults. *Journal of Consulting & Clinical Psychology, 67(6)*, 945-951.

Messman, T. L. & Long, P. J. (1996). Child sexual abuse and its relationship to revictimization in adult women: A review. *Clinical Psychology Review, 16*, 397-420.

Morris, J. (1997). Set free: Lesbian mental health and the coming out process. Unpublished dissertation.

Neisen, J. H. (1993). Healing from cultural victimization: Recovery from shame due to heterosexism. *Journal of Gay & Lesbian Psychotherapy, 2(1)*, 49-63.

Pharr, S. (1986). Two workshops on homophobia. In K. Lobel (Ed.), *Naming the violence (pp. 202-222). Seattle: Seal Press.*

Pharr, S. (1988). *Homophobia: A weapon of sexism.* Little Rock, AR: Chardon Press.

Renzetti, C. (1988). Violence in lesbian relationships: A preliminary analysis of causal factors. *Journal of Interpersonal Violence, 3(4)*, 381-399.

Renzetti, C. (1992). *Violent betrayal: Violence in lesbian relationships.* Thousand Oaks, CA: Sage.

Renzetti, C. (1995). Violence and abuse in lesbian relationships: Theoretical and empirical issues. In R. K. Bergen (Ed.), *Issues in intimate violence.* Thousand Oaks, CA: Sage.

Renzetti, C. (1999). The challenge to feminism posed by women's use of violence in intimate relationships. In S. Lamb, (Ed) *New versions of victims: Feminists struggle with the concept.* New York: New York University Press.

Sophie, J. (1987). Internalized homophobia and lesbian identity. *Journal of Homosexuality, 14*, 53-65.

Szymanski, D. M., & Chung, Y. B. (in press). The Lesbian Internalized Homophobia Scale: A rational/theoretical approach. *Journal of Homosexuality.*

Szymanski, D. M., Chung, Y. B., & Balsam, K. F. (in press). Psychosocial correlates of internalized homophobia in lesbians. *Measurement and Evaluation in Counseling and Development.*

Weinberg, G. (1972). *Society and the healthy homosexual.* New York: St. Martin's.

Knowledge About Heterosexual versus Lesbian Battering Among Lesbians

Erin M. McLaughlin
Patricia D. Rozee

SUMMARY. There is growing evidence to suggest that abuse in lesbian relationships does exist and may occur on a greater scale than most people are aware of. This paper will define battering in lesbian relationships, its prevalence and characteristics, critique the ability of traditional feminist models to explain lesbian battering, and address the consequent lack of community response to battered lesbians. We will also present results of a study indicating that the silence about lesbian battering among both feminist theorists and activists and the gay/lesbian community has contributed to the invisibility of lesbian battering, and thus lesbians' own lack of knowledge about lesbian battering. The results of this study support the hypothesis that the lesbian community is more familiar with phenomena associated with domestic violence in heterosexual relation-

---

Erin M. McLaughlin, MS, is a graduate of California State University, Long Beach's psychology program. She currently facilitates a co-gender domestic violence survivors' support group at the L.A. Gay and Lesbian Center, and works with women in prison.

Patricia D. Rozee, PhD, is Professor of Psychology and Women's Studies at California State University, Long Beach. She is a scholar, activist and teacher in the area of violence against women. Dr. Rozee has published extensively on sexual assault and rape resistance. She also teaches a course on "Women and Violence."

Address correspondence to: Patricia D. Rozee, 3556 California, Long Beach, CA 90807.

[Haworth co-indexing entry note]: "Knowledge About Heterosexual versus Lesbian Battering Among Lesbians." McLaughlin, Erin M., and Patricia D. Rozee. Co-published simultaneously in *Women & Therapy* (The Haworth Press, Inc.) Vol. 23, No. 3, 2001, pp. 39-58; and: *Intimate Betrayal: Domestic Violence in Lesbian Relationships* (ed: Ellyn Kaschak) The Haworth Press, Inc., 2001, pp. 39-58. Single or multiple copies of this article are available for a fee from The Haworth Document Delivery Service [1-800-342-9678, 9:00 a.m. - 5:00 p.m. (EST). E-mail address: getinfo@haworthpressinc.com].

39

ships than with violence in intimate lesbian relationships. Community and clinical implications of the findings are discussed. *[Article copies available for a fee from The Haworth Document Delivery Service: 1-800-342-9678. E-mail address: <getinfo@haworthpressinc.com> Website: <http://www.HaworthPress.com> © 2001 by The Haworth Press, Inc. All rights reserved.]*

KEYWORDS. Domestic violence, lesbian battering, same-sex violence

Within the scant research available, there is growing evidence to suggest that abuse in lesbian relationships does exist. Not only does this abuse reside within the lesbian community, but also it occurs on a greater scale than anyone in the gay or lesbian movement has acknowledged. This paper will define battering in lesbian relationships, its prevalence and characteristics, critique the ability of traditional feminist models to explain lesbian battering, and address the consequent lack of community response to battered lesbians. We will also present results of a study indicating that the silence about lesbian battering among both feminist theorists and activists and the gay/lesbian community has contributed to the invisibility of lesbian battering, and thus lesbians' own lack of knowledge about lesbian battering.

Relationship violence as it occurs for lesbians, is similar to the way it occurs for heterosexual women. Domestic violence in lesbian relationships involves almost identical patterns of physical, sexual and emotional abuse (Morrow & Hawxhurst, 1989). In her article on lesbian victims of intimate violence, Hammond (1989) defines battering as "a pattern of physical abuse or intimidation in which the batterer uses the actuality or threat of physical force, or violence, to exert control over the victim, thereby increasing the batterer's sense of power in the relationship" (p. 90). Physical battering itself can include a wide range of behaviors such as punching, kicking, rape, slapping, stabbing, hitting with objects, etc. One may think of woman-to-woman violence as less serious than males inflicting violence on females, but research contradicts this myth. As suggested by Hammond (1989), when this misconception is applied to battered lesbians, the impact of abuse in these relationships becomes misunderstood and minimized. To illustrate her assertion, Hammond (1989) points out that not only have battering experiences in lesbian relationships been intense enough to cause post-traumatic stress disorder, but also some lesbian batterers have killed their partners.

Lesbian relationships may, however, contain a higher rate of emotional abuse than heterosexual relationships (Brand & Kidd, 1986). Psychological abuse in violent lesbian relationships tends to be reported by researchers as more frequent than physical abuse (Renzetti, 1989; Renzetti, 1992; Lockhart, White, Causby & Isaac, 1994). This may be linked to the batterer's use of "outing" and homophobia to maintain power and control. For example, a lesbian's partner may threaten to expose the survivor's sexual orientation to homophobic family members if she attempts to leave the abusive relationship. The lesbian survivor of abuse may be unwilling to risk the possible loss of family members (because of exposure of her sexual orientation), giving the abuser a means of control in the relationship. Morrow and Hawxhurst (1989) concur with this statement, claiming that homophobic control is used by batterers in situations where they will tell their victims they deserve no better than to be abused or will never be able to find help because she is "just a lesbian." Hart (1986) asserts that the use of homophobic control by the batterer can extend to making statements about her victim not being a "real" lesbian because she had slept with men before. The message remains clear: both homosexual and heterosexual relationships have common aspects of batterers using violence, intimidation, and emotional abuse to exert power and control over their victims.

INCIDENCE AND PREVALENCE OF LESBIAN BATTERING

It is estimated that three to four million American heterosexual women are battered each year by their husbands or partners (Stark, 1981). We simply do not know the rate of battering in the lesbian community. Because of the stigmatization of lesbians in society, and the stigmatization of battered lesbians in the gay and lesbian community, non-random samples have been the only feasible way to accomplish research on battered lesbians (Renzetti, 1992). Such research, while informative about the process of lesbian battering from a survivor perspective, has not yet yielded practical prevalence information. Prevalence information that has been reported is highly subject to characteristics of methods of data collection in a given study, and often it is not clear whether incidence or prevalence is being reported (current vs. lifetime rates). Coleman (1994) reports rates from 25% to 52%, while a later review reports rates of 25% to 75% (see Waldner-Haugrud, Gratch, & Magruder, 1997, for an analysis of the issues). In contrast to the plethora of convenience studies on lesbian battering, one recent nationally representative sample found the lifetime prevalence of same-sex partner abuse was 11.4% versus 20.3% for opposite-sex partner abuse (Tjaden, Thoennes, & Allison, 1999). This study also notes that lesbians were more than twice as likely to report being victimized by male intimate partners than by females over their lifetime (30.4% vs. 11.4%).

TRADITIONAL FEMINIST MODELS OF BATTERING

Feminist theory is often used to guide interventions for battered women and to direct programs for men who batter them (Gelles, 1995). Services such as shelters, safe homes, support groups for survivors, and legal advocacy are typically created to meet the needs of women battered by male abusers (Hammond, 1989). The epistemology of domestic violence from some feminist perspectives considers battering to be a result of gender role inequality in heterosexual relationships. Liberal, social, radical, Marxist, and other feminist theorists differ on the origins of patriarchy and how it is perpetuated. Most would purport that patriarchy provides the structural and ideological support for male violence against women (Smith, 1990). This analysis becomes problematic when one takes into account both white battered lesbians and battered lesbians of color. Those working in the battered women's movement fought for society's recognition of battered women and of gender inequality. With the constant threat of losing recognition and credibility, the battered women's movement may not be quick to acknowledge battered lesbians because their presence challenges the analysis of gender inequality (Hammond, 1989). Traditional feminist analysis purports that domestic violence is created and perpetuated primarily by sexism in mainstream society. However, if one considers power structures as constant and emanating from multiple points, the one-sided and distorted nature of these analyses becomes apparent. Consequently, the application of the disparities in these analyses blocks white lesbians' and lesbians of colors' access to society's resources, resulting in the disempowerment of these individuals. It is probable that traditional feminist theories of battering have contributed to lack of acknowledgement of lesbian battering, as well as to lack of services to battered lesbians due to adherence of most domestic violence programs to traditional feminist explanatory models. What is needed is a new paradigm through which to view the phenomenon of domestic violence in our society. This paradigm should equally incorporate the issues of sexism, racism, homophobia, and heterosexism for a more encompassing understanding of domestic violence.

POWER AND BATTERING

Postmodernist feminist theory may also be helpful in reconceptualizing power for the purposes of understanding lesbian battering. Postmodernism refers to multiple centers of power, meanings of words, interpretations of reality, and identities so that there is a resistance towards universality in theory (Grant, 1993). This philosophy enables one to address power relations, gender, oppression, and freedom while avoiding essentialism. Power relations are considered constant, and emanating from multiple points within our social structure, as opposed to the critique of power as a monolithic structure, as exemplified in some feminist analyses of patriarchy (Grant, 1993). The postmodern feminist critique looks primarily at power relations, with gender as a sub-component of these relations. In other words, female oppression is only one out of many possible oppressions created by a web of power structures including, but not limited to, racism, sexism, capitalism, heterosexism, and homophobia. The interaction of gender systems with other power systems does not mean that all women experience gender as their primary oppression; nor do all women experience gender in the same way.

In order to fully understand lesbian battering, it is important to consider forms of power other than male dominance. Goode (1971) describes power as the ability to impose one's will upon another, with or without consent or resistance. Hence, force, or its threat, is merely one method among many to obtain compliance (Goode, 1971). Renzetti (1989) reports significant correlations between some indicators of power imbalance and violence in lesbian relationships. For example, class difference between partners was related to an increase in the number of abusive events in violent lesbian relationships (Renzetti, 1989). Further, Lockhart, White, Causby, and Isaac (1994) reported that physical abuse tended to be triggered by issues of power imbalance or a struggle for different levels of interdependence and autonomy in lesbian relationships. These studies confirm the results of Babcock, Waltz, Jacobson and Gottman (1993) who found that husbands' lower decision-making power, as assessed by the Who Does What Questionnaire (WDW), was related to increased violence. Babcock et al. (1993) suggest that when the husband is in a less powerful position than his wife, has a past history of physical violence, and possesses poor communication skills, the only effective method the perpetrator may have of asserting a dominant position might be through physical aggression. The use of power and control seems to be a common link among batterers regardless of circumstances of sexual orientation.

Renzetti (1992) found that differences in power-giving resources such as social class, intelligence, and earning power were not significant predictors of relationship violence for lesbians. Several researchers have suggested the importance of relational factors such as dependency and fusion or jealousy as causally related to lesbian battering (Renzetti, 1992; Waldner-Haugrud et al., 1997). Dutton (1994) suggests that intimacy generates dependency, jealousy and anger, and may result in violence in relationships. The lack of a substantive body of research on the issue precludes conclusions as to causality. But it is important to note that research on lesbian battering cautions us to expand our thinking past single explanatory factors of domestic violence toward more complex, multiply-determined explanations.

THE GAY AND LESBIAN COMMUNITY

The gay and lesbian community also veils lesbian battering in silence. This is apparent when considering that although battered lesbians are coming forward in alarmingly increasing numbers, the gay and lesbian community offers very few resources or acknowledgment in response. For example, the gay and lesbian community often does not have available hotlines for domestic violence, and generally no support groups for survivors of same sex violence, while there usually are resources for issues of alcoholism, co-dependency, networking, incest, and so on. Benowitz (1986) analyzes how homophobia affects the lesbian community's response to violence in lesbian relationships. She maintains that silence about abuse reflects an acute awareness of societal homophobia. By talking openly about lesbian battering, the lesbian community fears fueling society's hatred and myths about lesbians. Homophobia may affect the gay and lesbian community's response to lesbian battering because of the inherent belief that, by bringing up the subject of domestic violence in gay and lesbian relationships, what results is a negative reflection on the gay and lesbian community as a whole.

For the lesbian of color, the issue of lack of support from mainstream society may be further compounded by racism in the gay and lesbian community. Kanuha (1990) purports that lesbian culture is mainly represented in the cultural artifacts of music, art, and literature, which are supposed to represent the whole community. In actuality, representations have been predominantly of white lesbian culture. As a part of larger society, lesbian culture is not excluded from being affected by racism. This racism is evident in the absence of lesbians of color perspectives in social, political, economic, and academic institutions. For example, as of 1992 only two published studies on anti-lesbian and anti-gay victimization and violence have examined racial and ethnic differences in rates of victimization (Herek & Berrill, 1992). Both found that lesbians and gays of color are at a greater risk for violent attack because of their sexual orientation. This lack of attention to lesbian and gay men of color issues may be related to a tendency for the gay and lesbian community to consider homophobia as the main oppression its members must face, thus minimizing the important interconnections among racism, sexism, and homophobia (Kanuha, 1990).

The gay and lesbian community may also have their own myths surrounding lesbian relationships. These include the myth of the "utopia" of lesbian relationships, where women do not oppress, and certainly do not beat up, other women. Hammond (1989) suggests that lesbians may also internalize sexist stereotypes, which imply women are not big or strong enough to really hurt each other. Feminist/lesbian communities can make it especially difficult for abuse victims to find help because of the belief in the myth that lesbian relationships are egalitarian, loving, and passionate, but never violent (Morrow & Hawxhurst, 1989).

Caldwell and Peplau (1984) reported that although a majority of the lesbians in their research (97%) expressed support for the ideal of equal power in their relationships, 39% reported an imbalance in power, where one partner had greater resources (such as higher education or income) than the other. Lesbians were defined as unequal in status if they were more involved in the relationship than their partner, and if they had less education or income than the partner did (Caldwell & Peplau, 1984). Reilly and Lynch (1990) found in their survey of 70 lesbian couples that although egalitarianism was the ideal in most relationships, this ideal had not been achieved to that degree. These researchers found that 55% of the subjects surveyed perceived an actual power imbalance. For those couples who agreed a power inequity existed in their relationships, a significant disparity was found in financial assets (Reilly & Lynch, 1990).

The gay and lesbian community is very close-knit in terms of its circle of socialization. Friends often support the lesbian and become like family, which is important because lesbians may lose their own families as a result of prejudice against their sexual orientation. If the battered lesbian chooses to end her relationship with the abuser, she may lose "custody" of the friends, and hence lose her own support system (Hammond, 1989). Also, the lesbian community can be so small that the battered lesbian may not feel safe in many gay or lesbian establishments, or events, because of a high probability that she may encounter her abuser (Hammond, 1989). The need for safety and support systems for battered lesbians may be greater than for battered heterosexual women, because of the nature of these close-knit communities.

THE PURPOSE OF STUDY

The purpose of this study was to investigate the idea that the lesbian community may not be conceptualizing violence in lesbian relationships as domestic violence. Due to predominant feminist theories of battering, lack of training about gay/lesbian issues, invisibility of lesbian battering both in the lesbian/gay community and the larger community, absence of resources for battered lesbians, and other factors, there simply may not be enough information for lesbians to parallel the cycle of violence portrayed in heterosexual battering relationships to lesbian battering relationships. Thus, lesbians will tend to internalize the dominant heterosexual paradigms of domestic violence within their community. Since most domestic violence discourse is written from a "male-as-batterer" perspective, lesbians can be expected to perceive domestic violence within a mainstream paradigm including violence in their own relationships. Our hypothesis was that lesbians would be more familiar with the dynamics associated with domestic violence in heterosexual relationships than with the dynamics of domestic violence in lesbian relationships when identical phenomena are associated with each type of violence.

METHOD

Participants

The participants in this study were 297 lesbians/bisexual women within a large urban southwestern county. Surveys were distributed in front of the Gay and Lesbian Center and during the annual Gay Pride event. Participants were asked to volunteer to take part in a study about dynamics within intimate relationships.

INSTRUMENTS

Battered Woman Questionnaire

Dodge and Greene's (1991) *Battered Woman Questionnaire* (BWQ) was used to assess the lesbian community's knowledge of domestic violence in intimate relationships. The BWQ contains 18 items that were created to assess knowledge and beliefs about different aspects of domestic violence. Dodge and Greene (1991) surveyed the responses of 45 researchers, considered to be experts in the domestic violence field, to each item on the BWQ. This study found a high level of agreement among the researchers in response to items on the questionnaire, and established this consensus as an empirical measure of knowledge. Most items on the BWQ relate to aspects of the *Battered Woman Syndrome* (Walker, 1984) for which there is a general scientific concurrence in the domestic violence research literature. For example, scientific consensus supports that battered women may experience feelings of helplessness and self-blame (Greene, Raitz, & Lindblad, 1989). Other items on the questionnaire relate to Walker's (1984) contentions that the general public subscribes to myths about battered women.

Two versions developed from the BWQ were used to test the lesbian community's knowledge of domestic violence. The first version, the "Heterosexual Battered Woman Questionnaire" (HBWQ), consisted of the original 18 BWQ items. The second, the "Lesbian Battered Woman Questionnaire" (LBWQ), was a modified version of the first 18 items of the HBWQ, which replaced the term "battered woman" with "lesbian in a violent intimate relationship," and used the term "partner" to replace the term "husband." The term, "a lesbian who is a survivor of a violent intimate relationship," was used to denote the difference between perpetrator and survivor in questionnaire items.

PROCEDURE

Upon agreeing to participate in the study, all participants signed a consent form. Participants were given the demographic questionnaire assessing sexual orientation, personal experiences with domestic violence, age, income, education and ethnicity, and either the HBWQ or the LBWQ using random distribution. Volunteers completed all materials on clipboards at the distribution sites. A debriefing statement, containing information about gay and lesbian domestic violence, as well as community resources, was given to participants immediately after they completed the questionnaires.

RESULTS

Demographic Information. The demographic section showed that the sample adequately represents the demographics of the general population from which the sample was drawn. Respondents were 51% Caucasian, 20% Latina, 13% African American, 6% Asian American, 1% American Indian, and 9% other. A majority of respondents were between the ages of 18 and 33 (54.3%), 23.2% were between the ages of 34 and 41, and 23.2% were 42 or over. The sexual orientation of the sample was as follows: 41 were bisexual (of which 66% were women of color) and 256 lesbians (of which 47% were women of color). Respondents tended to be fairly well educated, 46% reported between one and three years of higher education, and 19% reported possessing a bachelor's degree. A majority of respondents were in the middle-income level: 18.3% of respondents made between $0 and $8,000 annually, 32.8% made between $17,000 and $32,000, and 19% made $45,000 or more per year.

Experience with Battering. Questions regarding personal experiences with violence in intimate relationships were also assessed. Respondents reported experiences with domestic violence in both lesbian and heterosexual relationships. Sixty-nine percent of respondents reported knowing a victim of violence in a lesbian relationship. Eighty-seven percent reported knowing a victim of violence in a heterosexual relationship. Thirty-four percent reported having been a victim of violence in a lesbian relationship, and 25% reported having been a victim of heterosexual relationship violence. Twelve percent of respondents reported that they had been victims of domestic violence in both heterosexual and lesbian relationships.

Responses to questionnaire items were tested for significant differences between groups on the basis of reported personal experience with domestic violence. Analyses revealed that there was little difference in response to questionnaire items between subjects who experienced violence and those who did not, regardless of whether or not that violence took place in a heterosexual or lesbian context. The only question on which battered women and non-battered women differed concerned the woman leaving her batterer. Whether heterosexual or lesbian, battered women were less likely to say that the woman could just leave her batterer.

Relationship Between the HBWQ and LBWQ. The differences between responses to the Heterosexual Battered Women's Questionnaire (HBWQ), and Lesbian Battered Women's Questionnaire (LBWQ) were analyzed using a t-test. Results showed a significant difference between the two groups (t (295) = 4.062, p = .000). Respondents tended to endorse items (both agreeing and disagreeing) more strongly on the Battered Women's Questionnaire than on the Lesbian Battered Women's Questionnaire. This indicates that the lesbian community was much more likely to demonstrate knowledge regarding the dynamics of domestic violence in a heterosexual relationship than within lesbian relationships. Respondents agreed that a battered woman might believe that her husband could kill her; a battered woman might stay with her husband because she feels dependent on him; a battered woman might be persuaded to stay with her husband if he promised never to hurt her again; most battered women believe that they are helpless to stop the violence; a woman in an abusive situation might blame herself for the violence in the relationship; and battered women might believe that using deadly force against their husbands is the only way for them to stay alive. The lesbian community did not apply the same strong endorsements to battered lesbians in replicated situations.

DISCUSSION

The purpose of this study was to test the hypothesis that lesbians may not be conceptualizing violence in lesbian relationships as domestic violence in the same way as they do domestic violence in heterosexual relationships. The results of this study support the hypothesis that the lesbian community is more familiar with phenomena associated with domestic violence in heterosexual relationships than with violence in intimate lesbian relationships. These findings may indicate that although the lesbian community shows considerable knowledge about domestic violence in heterosexual relationships, this same knowledge may not be transferred as strongly to violence in intimate lesbian relationships. Theoretical models, training, research and community practices surrounding domestic violence in social helping institutions may contribute to a lack of information for lesbians to parallel the cycle of violence portrayed in heterosexual relationships to lesbian battering relationships. The ways in which the battered women's movement has applied traditional feminist analyses of domestic violence have contributed to narrow conceptualizations of violent relationships by society's helping institutions. Lesbians do not tend to fit within traditional feminist analyses of the "battered woman," which primarily focuses upon theories of male dominance. Thus, new models to explain lesbian battering must be considered. Such models will require more complex analysis of the etiology of battering such that multicausal models can better explain lesbian battering.

Service providers need to use strategies to make their services more sensitive to the needs of lesbians in violent relationships. Renzetti (1996) suggests that there should be training for staff on lesbian battering, specific policies to address homophobia among staff, volunteers, and clients, use of inclusive language, and outreach to the gay and lesbian community through programming, advertising, and community education/media campaigns. Conducting sensitivity training on homophobia, examining service protocols for heterosexist language within battered women's shelters, and holding community forums on lesbian battering are all strategies that could lead to the empowerment of survivors (Hammond, 1989).

Access to Resources

Lesbians who are survivors of domestic violence not only need access to resources, but service providers who are adequately equipped to respond to lesbian issues. Several researchers have found that such resources and service providers are hard to find. In 1996, Renzetti conducted a survey of domestic violence resources available for, and sensitive to, battered lesbians through the 1991 National Directory of Domestic Violence Programs. From a return of 566 questionnaires, Renzetti found that only 9.7% of service providers reported outreach efforts specifically targeting lesbian victims. Efforts included things such as distributing brochures on lesbian battering, advertising services in lesbian/gay newspapers or other media, and offering support groups for battered lesbians. Further, only 47.9% reported that their staff received specific training on domestic violence in lesbian relationships.

Homophobia may disempower battered lesbians by limiting their ability to access social resources, such as shelters, hotlines, or support groups for help in domestic violence situations. Lie and Gentlewarrier (1991) found that a majority of lesbian respondents, who experienced abuse in their relationships, indicated that they were unlikely to use resources such as shelters, support groups and medical services. This was thought by the researchers to be a result of the real and perceived homophobia and heterosexism of the mainstream community service units and providers, which cause unresponsiveness and insensitivity to the needs of battered lesbians (Lie & Gentlewarrier, 1991). For example, lesbians have been refused shelter for battering situations solely on the basis of their sexuality, and domestic violence hotlines often assume the heterosexuality of lesbians calling for help. Renzetti (1989) found that many sources of formal help, frequently available to heterosexual victims, are not perceived by lesbian victims to be resources of aid available to them. Few people in Renzetti's study sought help from hotlines and women's shelters. Of those seeking assistance, resources were reported to be either no help at all or only a little helpful (Renzetti, 1989).

Training of Helping Professionals. Heterosexism, the belief of the superiority and normalcy of being heterosexual (Lorde, 1983), enforces the invisibility of homosexuals and bisexuals through the assumption that everyone is heterosexual. Heterosexism's enforcement of invisibility is demonstrated through the absence of educational or training programs for those working in human service fields. For example, most educational programs lack specific course work and training on gay, lesbian, and bisexual issues. In 1989, a nationwide survey of counselor education programs found that fewer than 10% of counselors were required to take a course in sexuality (Harbeck, 1992). Further, surveying doctoral programs approved by the American Psychological Association, Harbeck found that only 37% offered a graduate course in human sexuality. Within the medical field, a 1991 survey of four-year medical schools in the United States found the mean amount of course time devoted to the topic of homosexuality was 3 hours, 26 minutes (Wallick, 1992). In 1991, it was estimated that a total of no more than 20 professionals in four different American cities were adequately experienced or trained to deal effectively with lesbian and gay victims of domestic violence (Island, 1991). This statistic is particularly staggering considering that domestic violence is cited as the third largest health problem facing gay men today (Island, 1991). This is second only to substance abuse and AIDS (Island, 1991).

Legal Systems. In coping with police, lawyers, and judges, the battered lesbian may have to contend not only with a system not totally sympathetic to battering situations in general, but also with one that is racist, homophobic, and heterosexist. Kanuha (1990) maintains that because of institutionalized racism, people of color are wary of admitting to "mainstream" white society that domestic violence exists in their communities. Lesbians of color not only have problems seeking help due to fear of reprisal from white society, but also from homophobia within their own ethnic communities. Because of the powerful effect of sexism and homophobia throughout society in general, many people of color blame the existence of lesbians on white feminists (Kanuha, 1990). In order to protect themselves from increased racist attacks from white society, Kanuha (1990) asserts that people of color designate lesbians as "White-ness" and dissociate themselves from "social deviants" that white people do not even want to have among them (p. 175). Because of this homophobia, lesbians of color may choose not to disclose their sexual identity within their ethnic communities. Within our sample, women of color were more likely to describe themselves as bisexual rather than lesbian.

Castillo (1991) suggests if a Latina has less education and privilege than her Anglo counterparts, feels uncomfortable with the language of the dominant culture, and feels alienated from that culture, she is less likely to challenge the social mores of her ethnic community. Castillo (1991) states, "Above all, I believe, they [Latina lesbians] do not want to lose the love and sense of place they feel within their families and immediate communities. In light of intense Anglo alienation, this is a crucial aspect of their sense of identity" (p. 38). Therefore, with added discrimination from the ethnic community that has typically sheltered them from racism, lesbians of color may feel reluctant to seek help because of the threat of homophobic attacks and rejection from one of the few support networks available.

Homophobia and heterosexism within helping networks occur on many levels. Based on observations from her clinical practice, Hammond (1989) indicates that police called to handle an abusive episode between two women may minimize the danger the victim is in, behave in a physically intrusive manner, make homophobic comments, and fail to make appropriate referrals to available resources. Renzetti (1989) found that some subjects stated official help providers responded negatively to them instead of giving support, or confronting the batterer. As an example, Renzetti (1989) noted one subject, who reported a negative experience with a police officer responding to her call for help. This person was insulted by the officer, who called her a "queer devil," and who told the subject she deserved trouble because she was a lesbian (p. 160). Police, enforcing heterosexist laws, may charge perpetrators with battery, as opposed to domestic violence. This lack of inclusion or recognition may prevent lesbians from accessing available services for help.

Lesbians may also have to deal with laws that are heterosexist, and which provide little or no protection for them. Robson (1992) contends that feminists worked to force the legal system to recognize domestic violence in the context of marriage. Legal reforms were made, such as the battered wife's defense for the protection of battered wives. However, in the legal sense, this defense tends only to apply to heterosexual women (Robson, 1992). A battered lesbian may not be entitled to any legal relief in a state that does not consider her within the statutory definition of a victim of domestic violence. Robson (1992) uses the example of the state of Florida, where the definition of domestic violence is limited to: "any assault, battery or sexual battery by a person against the person's spouse or against any other person related by blood or marriage to the petitioner, or respondent, who is residing in the same single dwelling unit" (p. 160).

Judges who support battered women may still perpetuate myths about battered lesbians (Hammond, 1989). Battering in these relationships is often believed by judges to be mutual. Mutual battering can be defined as both partners in a relationship acting equally as perpetrators and survivors of abuse. As a result of lack of education about same-sex domestic violence, and consequent confusion about exactly who is the perpetrator in violent lesbian relationships, judges may provide batterers with legal sanctions (Hammond, 1989). Another element in this confusion may be that the survivors themselves feel guilty about using violence in self-defense against their partners. Victims may be unclear about whether they were aggressors or victims when they resorted to aggression . . . even if it was to defend themselves (Leeder, 1988; Bush, Lie, Montagne, Reyes, & Schilit, 1991). In lesbian battering situations, there is a need to talk to both parties in the relationship. The situation usually is not mutual combat, and interviewers need to probe for who is in control within the relationship. Within the field of research on domestic violence, there are strong conclusions that the idea of mutual combat is not supported (Renzetti, 1992). However, as addressed in the literature review, mainstream service providers, as well as survivors of domestic violence themselves, seem to be more confused about the idea of mutual combat. Because there is not a visible perpetrator who fits within the mainstream interpretation of what a batterer looks like, one has to look more towards issues of power and control within lesbian relationships.

Medical Systems. The institution of medical services may also be threatening to the battered lesbian for many reasons connected to racism, heterosexism and homophobia. The lesbian seeking medical help may be faced with decisions to "come out" both as a battered woman and as a lesbian. Should she choose not to "come out," the medical staff may recognize her injuries as ones resulting from domestic violence, but assume the batterer is male (Hammond,

1989). On the other hand, if the victim of domestic violence does identify herself as a lesbian, she may risk the recording of such information in her medical file.

Smith, Heaton and Siever (1990) identified risks and fears of coming out to health-care providers. Among these fears, many lesbians were concerned that health-care providers would violate their trust and confidentiality. Another study by Zeidenstein (1990) found one-fourth of lesbians responding to a questionnaire stated they would not come out to their health care provider if their medical records would reflect their sexual orientation.

Some lesbians of color may experience problems when attempting to utilize medical services, because of language barriers. For example, if the survivor speaks only Spanish, and medical personnel do not speak this language, the already delicate communications surrounding domestic violence in lesbian relationships may be further complicated. Racism and stereotyping of cultures could be further perpetuated in conjunction with heterosexism. For example, medical personnel, recognizing these injuries to be ones of domestic violence, may assume this is due to cultural norms surrounding issues of "machismo" in males. The assumption of both heterosexuality and stereotypes of what one believes may be a cultural norm serves to minimize and compound an already difficult issue for the battered lesbian of color.

The lesbian survivor of domestic violence may also have problems with services provided by battered women's shelters and/or programs. In seeking help from shelters or hotlines, the same racism, heterosexism, and homophobia may be apparent here as with the legal and medical systems. Leeder (1988) comments on this lack of support, acknowledging most battered women's shelters do not provide support for lesbians. Staff working in the shelters, as well as the other residents living in the shelters, may think the lesbian survivor deserved what she got because of the belief in the inherent abnormality of homosexuality (Hammond, 1989). The same problems exist with staff working hotlines, support groups, and crisis counseling.

Several researchers also address the necessity of providing culturally competent domestic violence services to lesbians. Social service agencies must consider the specific needs of different communities when planning outreach programs (Waldron, 1996). For example, advertising only in gay and lesbian newspapers may not be adequate when attempting to reach gays and lesbians of color. Service providers may also want to advertise in local papers of different ethnic communities. Further, social service providers need to network within communities of color. Organizers and leaders who have the recognition and respect of community members as people who are resources of non-traditional help should be utilized (Waldron, 1996). In terms of making services accessible to a diverse population, those providing direct services should reflect the characteristics of the population they aim to serve (Mendez, 1996). There is also a need for culturally diverse support groups and the availability of multi-language materials/staff.

Clinical Interventions. When social service providers/clinicians are working directly with survivors of domestic violence in lesbian relationships, a myriad of concerns should be addressed. The results of this research indicate that it is unlikely that lesbian clients will recognize the physical violence and/or emotional abuse within their relationships as domestic violence. Therefore, social service providers/clinicians need to be aware of, and directly probe for, this information. As suggested by Hammond (1989), clinical intakes should have questions that specifically screen for domestic violence. Within these intakes, the extent and severity of abuse or battering should be assessed, as well as the lethality of the abusive relationship. Elements of the lethality of the batterer should include whether she/he owns a weapon, stalking behaviors, threats to take the life of the survivor, threats of batterer to take her/his own life, is the violence increasing in frequency and severity, and so on.

Researchers have found that the most dangerous time for survivors of domestic violence is when first they leave their batterers. U.S. Department of Justice statistics in 1986 have shown that 70% of domestic violence occurs after the relationship has ended (Stahly, 2000). Further, most homicides that involve domestic violence occur when survivors leave their batterers (Hammond, 1989; Stahly, 2000). In light of such danger, one of the most important aspects of working with survivors within a social services/clinical setting is their safety. Therapists should be knowledgeable of safety planning not only for survivors who have just left their batterers, but also for ones still within their relationships. Safety planning should include such things as planning escape routes in the areas the batterer could be encountered, information about restraining orders, changing locks in a household, informing neighbors and co-workers of the domestically violent situation, changing regular travelling patterns, parking cars in hidden locations, etc. Particularly for survivors who choose to remain with the batterer, social service providers should teach the survivor how to assess and act on the degree of lethality in their situation (Peled, Eisikovits, Enosh, & Winstok, 2000).

Lesbian survivors of domestic violence often experience intense isolation. A part of emotional abuse that batterers typically perpetrate against survivors includes cutting them off from friends, family, and people in the outside world. Homophobia implemented as a method of power and control often compounds isolation, particularly if the survivor is not "out" (identified as a lesbian to others), or if friends and/or family have abandoned her already as a result of her sexual orientation. The batterer may use the threat of exposing the survivor's sexual orientation as a method of controlling her. For example, the batterer may threaten to tell the survivor's boss she is a lesbian, risking her employment, if she does not do as she is told (Burstow, 1992). As a clinician/social service provider, another important part of empowering a survivor may include assisting her with establishing a support network and reducing the sense of isolation (Burstow, 1992; Morrow & Hawxhurst, 1989).

At first, the therapist/social service provider may be the only system of support available for the lesbian survivor of domestic violence (Lie & Gentlewarrier, 1991). Familiarization with outside resources, such as gay and lesbian centers, shelters, hotlines, low cost/free individual counseling, support groups, domestic assault response teams, and legal aide, is crucial to supporting domestic violence survivors. Therapists may also have to advocate for survivors by initiating training shelter staff and identifying shelters that are lesbian-sensitive (Burstow, 1992; Morrow & Hawxhurst, 1989).

Part of empowering battered lesbians includes not only conducting outreach, education, safety planning and networking, but also avoiding re-victimizing survivors as social service providers. Service providers should take conscious precautions to safeguard survivors' confidentiality, particularly as it relates to their sexual orientation. In many environments, lesbians whose sexual orientation becomes known to others risk the loss of things such as their employment, residence, and children (Garnets, Herek, & Levy, 1990).

Couples counseling should be avoided when domestic violence is present. Couples counseling can escalate the violence in the relationships and put the survivor at risk (Morrow & Hawxhurst, 1989). The batterer oftentimes uses what the survivor expresses in couples therapy as ammunition to abuse her, and consequently, the survivor does not have a safe environment within the therapeutic context to express herself. Similarly, a batterer and survivor should not see the same therapist in individual counseling (Morrow & Hawxhurst, 1989). The same dynamics that occur in couples counseling for domestically violent partners tend to occur with couples who have the same individual counselor. For example, batterers may use real or perceived disclosures in therapy as ammunition to attack the survivor.

Therapists and social service providers should become well-versed not only with the cycle of abuse, dynamics of power and control, and the multiple points of power relations (sexism, heterosexism, homophobia and racism), but be prepared to educate survivors regarding them. Above all else the provider must be aware of any misconceptions he/she may have about battered lesbians. For example, the myth that violence within lesbian relationships is less serious than violence perpetrated by males upon females may result in a minimization of the violence the survivor is experiencing, and may put the battered lesbian at risk. Acknowledgement of the extent and severity of the violence the battered lesbian survived, as well as navigating the survivor through PTSD symptoms, may be an important part of the path to recovery.

Community psychologist Julian Rappaport (1981) advocated a "pursuit of paradox" in his field of research. This pursuit incorporated looking for contradictions in theory, or finding places in social and community institutions that have become one-sided, with the purpose of changing them to encompass a more empowering solution. Rappaport's assertions seem particularly relevant to the field of domestic violence. The ways in which the battered women's movement has applied traditional feminist analyses of domestic violence has contributed to narrow conceptualizations of violent relationships by society's helping institutions. The case of the battered lesbian is prima facie evidence that battering is not created and perpetuated only by sexism in mainstream society. Institutionalized racism, heterosexism, and homophobia permeate the battered lesbian's experience with police, lawyers, judges, medical personnel, and domestic violence shelters. If one considers power structures as constant and emanating from multiple points, the one-sided and distorted nature of these analyses becomes apparent. New, more complex and encompassing models are needed to truly impact the incidence of battering in women's lives.

REFERENCES

Babcock, J.C., Waltz, J., Jacobson, N.S., & Gottman, J.M. (1993). Power and violence: The relation between communication patterns, power discrepancies, and domestic violence. *Journal of Consulting and Clinical Psychology, 61*(1), 40-50.

Benowitz, M. (1986). How homophobia affects lesbians' response to violence in lesbian relationships. In K. Lobel (Ed.), *Naming the violence: Speaking out about lesbian battering* (pp. 198-201). Seattle: The Seal Press.

Brand, P.A., & Kidd, A.H. (1986). Frequency of physical aggression in heterosexual and female homosexual dyads. *Psychological Reports, 59*(1), 1307-1313.

Burstow, B. (1992). *Radical feminist therapy.* Newbury Park: Sage Publications.

Bush, J., Lie, G.Y., Montagne, M., Reyes, L., & Schilit, R. (1991). Lesbians in currently aggressive relationships: How frequently do they report aggressive past relationships? *Violence and Victims, 6*(2), 121-135.

Caldwell, M.A., & Peplau, L.A. (1984). The balance of power in lesbian relationships. *Sex Roles, 10*(7/8), 587-599.

Castillo, A. (1991) La macha. Towards a beautiful self. In C. Trujillo (Ed.), *Chicana lesbians: The girls our mother warned us about* (pp. 24-48). Berkeley, CA: Third Woman Press.

Coleman, V.E. (1994). Lesbian battering: The relationship between personality and the perpetration of violence. *Violence and Victims, 9*(2), 139-152.

Dodge, M., & Greene, E. (1991). Juror and expert conceptions of battered women. *Violence and Victims, 6*(4), 271-282.

Dutton, D.F. (1994). Patriarchy and wife assault: The ecological fallacy. *Violence and Victims, 9*(2), 167-182.

Garnets, L., Herek, G.M., & Levy, B. (1990). Violence and victimization of lesbians and gay men. *Journal of Interpersonal Violence, 5*(3), 366-383.

Gelles, R.J. (1995). The nature of the problem of family violence. Paper presented for the Committee on the Assessment of Family Violence Interventions National Research Council.

Goode, W.J. (1971). Force and violence in the family. *Journal of Marriage and the Family, 33*(4), 624-635.

Grant, J. (1993). *Fundamental feminism.* New York: Routledge.

Greene, E., Raitz, A., & Lindblad, H. (1989). Jurors' knowledge of battered women. *Journal of Family Violence, 4*(2), 105-125.

Hammond, N. (1989). Lesbian victims of relationship violence. *Women & Therapy, 8*(1/2), 89-105.

Harbeck, K.M. (1992). *Coming out of the classroom closet: Gay and lesbian students, teachers, and curricula.* New York: Harrington Park Press.

Hart, B. (1986). Lesbian battering: An examination. In K. Lobel (Ed.), *Naming the violence: Speaking out about lesbian battering* (pp. 173-189). Seattle: The Seal Press.

Herek, G.M., & Berrill, K.T. (1992). *Hate crimes: Confronting violence against lesbians and gay men.* Newbury Park: Sage Press.

Island, D. (1991). *Men who beat the men who love them: Battered gay men and domestic violence.* New York: Harrington Park Press.

Kanuha, V. (1990). Compounding the triple jeopardy: Battering in lesbian of color relationships. *Women & Therapy, 8*(1/2), 169-184.

Leeder, E. (1988). Enmeshed in pain: Counseling the lesbian battering couple. *Women & Therapy, 7*(1), 81-99.

Lie, G.W., & Gentlewarrier, S. (1991). Intimate violence in lesbian relationships: Discussion of survey findings and practice implications. *Journal of Social Service Research, 15*(1/2), 41-59.

Lockhart, L.L., White, B.W., Causby, V., & Isaac, A. (1994). Letting out the secret: Violence in lesbian relationships. *Journal of Interpersonal Violence, 9*(4), 469-492.

Lorde, A. (1983). The master's tools will never dismantle the master's house. In G. Anzaldua & C. Moraga (Eds.), *This bridge called my back: Writings by radical women of color* (pp. 98-101). New York: Kitchen Table: Women of Color Press.

Mendez, J. (1996). Serving gays and lesbians of color who are survivors of domestic violence. *Journal of Gay & Lesbian Social Services, 4*(1), 53-59.

Morrow, S.L., & Hawxhurst, D.M. (1989). Lesbian partner abuse: Implications for therapists. *Journal of Counseling & Development, 68,* 58-62.

Peled, E., Eisikovita, Z., Enosh, G., & Winstok, Z. (2000). Choice and empowerment for battered women who stay: Toward a constructivist model. *Social Work, 45*(1), 9-25.

Rappaport, J. (1981). In praise of paradox: A social policy of empowerment over prevention. *American Journal of Community Psychology, 9, (1), 1-25.*

Reilly, M.E., & Lynch, J.M. (1990). Power sharing in lesbian partnerships. *Journal of Homosexuality, 19*(3), 1-28.

Renzetti, C.M. (1988). Building a second closet: Third party responses to victims of lesbian partner abuse. *Family Relations, 38*, 157-163.

Renzetti, C.M. (1992). *Violent betrayal: Partner abuse in lesbian relationships.* Newbury Park: Sage Publications, Inc.

Renzetti, C. (1996). The poverty of services for battered lesbians. *Journal of Gay & Lesbian Social Services, 4*(1), 61-68.

Robson, R. (1992). *Lesbian (Out)law: Survival under the rule of law.* New York: Firebrand Books.

Smith, M.D. (1990). Patriarchal ideology and wife beating: A test of a feminist hypothesis. *Violence and Victims, 5*(4), 257-273.

Smith, M., Heaton, C., & Siever, D. (1990). Health concerns of lesbians. *Physician Assistant, 14*(1), 81-94.

Stahly, G.B. (2000). Battered women: Why don't they just leave? In J.C. Chrisler, C. Golden, & P.D. Rozee (Eds.), *Lectures on the psychology of women* (pp. 288-305). Boston: McGraw-Hill Higher Education.

Stark, E. (1981). *Wife abuse in the medical setting: An introduction for health personnel* (Monograph Series No. 7, National Clearing House on Domestic Violence). Washington, DC: U.S. Government Printing Office.

Tjaden, P., Thoennes, N., & Allison, C.S. (1999). Comparing violence over the life span in samples of same-sex and opposite-sex cohabitants. *Violence and Victims, 14*(4), 413-425.

Waldner-Haugrud, L.K., Gratch, L.V., & Magruder, B. (1997). Victimization and perpetration rates of violence in gay and lesbian relationships: Gender issues explored. *Violence and Victims, 12*(2), pp. 173-184.

Waldron, C. (1996). Lesbians of color and the domestic violence movement. *Journal of Gay & Lesbian Social Services, 4*(1), 43-51.

Walker, L.E. (1984). *The battered woman syndrome.* New York: Springer.

Wallick, M. (1992). How the subject of homosexuality is taught at U.S. medical schools. *Academic Medicine, 67.*

Zeidenstein, L. (1990). Gynecological and childbearing needs of lesbians. *Journal of Nurse-Midwifery, 35*(1), 10-16.

Decentering Heterosexuality: Responses of Feminist Counselors to Abuse in Lesbian Relationships

Janice L. Ristock

SUMMARY. This paper reports on research involving eight focus group discussions with seventy feminist counselors who respond in their work to abuse in lesbian relationships. Focus group discussions allowed for information to be gathered on their observations about same-sex partner abuse and at the same time provided occasion for critical reflexivity.

Janice L. Ristock is Associate Professor, Women's Studies Program, University of Manitoba.

This research was supported by a grant from the Lesbian Health Fund of the Gay and Lesbian Medical Association and from the Social Sciences and Humanities Research Council of Canada. Many thanks to Vycki Anastasiadis, Caroline Fusco, Cindy Holmes, Natasha Hurley, Jan Mitchell and Betsy Szilock who worked as research assistants on the project.

Also, thanks to the Rainbow Resource Centre in Winnipeg; The FREDA Centre for Research on Violence Against Women and Children, Battered Women's Support Services, and The Centre for GLBT's and Allies in Vancouver; The David Kelley GLBT Counseling Program and Women's Health in Women's Hands in Toronto; the Sexual Assault Centre in London, Ontario; Peer Support Services for Battered Women in Calgary; and the Avalon Sexual Assault Centre in Halifax, Nova Scotia for providing the author with space and contacts, and advertising this research. Special thanks to Myrna Carlsen, Laurie Chesley, Karlene Faith, Donna Huen, Yasmin Jiwani, Louise MacPherson, Marg McGill, Kathleen O'Connell, Jane Oxenbury, Donna Wilson, Rae-Ann Woods. The author is grateful to Catherine Taylor for her editorial comments and ongoing support.

Address correspondence to: Janice L. Ristock, Women's Studies Program, University of Manitoba, Winnipeg, Manitoba, Canada, R3T 2N2 (E-mail: ristock@cc.umanitoba.ca).

[Haworth co-indexing entry note]: "Decentering Heterosexuality: Responses of Feminist Counselors to Abuse in Lesbian Relationships." Ristock, Janice L. Co-published simultaneously in *Women & Therapy* (The Haworth Press, Inc.) Vol. 23, No. 3, 2001, pp. 59-72; and: *Intimate Betrayal: Domestic Violence in Lesbian Relationships* (ed: Ellyn Kaschak) The Haworth Press, Inc., 2001, pp. 59-72. Single or multiple copies of this article are available for a fee from The Haworth Document Delivery Service [1-800-342-9678, 9:00 a.m. - 5:00 p.m. (EST). E-mail address: getinfo@haworthpressinc.com].

The focus groups illustrate how thoroughly we rely on heteronormative discourses and feminist categories and constructs to think about violence, and how these can impede our efforts to understand and respond effectively to same-sex partner abuse. Overall, the paper encourages more opportunities for group discussion among counselors so that we can share important insights into same-sex partner abuse and encourage a critical analysis of therapeutic practices and the normative assumptions behind them. *[Article copies available for a fee from The Haworth Document Delivery Service: 1-800-342-9678. E-mail address: <getinfo@haworthpressinc. com> Website: <http://www.HaworthPress.com> © 2001 by The Haworth Press, Inc. All rights reserved.]*

KEYWORDS. Lesbian partner abuse, feminist counselors, focus groups, discourse analysis

Over the last 15 years we have seen more and more research being done on the issue of lesbian partner violence and more broadly, on same-sex domestic violence (e.g., Leventhal & Lundy, 1999; Lobel, 1986; Renzetti, 1992; Renzetti & Miley, 1996). Many of these reports include discussions about a lack of social services available to lesbians and gay men. They report on the barriers gays and lesbians experience when accessing services, such as perceived or actual homophobia (Turell, 1999) and racism (Kanuha, 1990); and they comment on the inability of most services to respond fully to same-sex partner violence because of mainstream heterosexual approaches and assumptions (Ristock, 1994; Ristock, 1997; Russo, 1999). Several survey studies report that lesbians who do access formal services are more likely to turn to counselors for therapy than to call the police, use the criminal justice system, access health care services or turn to shelters for battered women (Renzetti, 1992; Ristock, 1998; Scherzer, 1998; Turell, 1999). Susan Turell (1999) sees the popularity of counseling as the response to relationship violence as a troubling one. In her survey of 499 ethnically diverse gay, lesbian, bisexual, transgendered people (GLBT) she asked a hypothetical question about what services are most needed for people in abusive relationships. Over two thirds mentioned some form of counseling (i.e., individual, support groups, self-help). In Turell's view, this suggests that gays and lesbians think of relationship abuse as a personal, private issue needing an intrapsychic response rather than seeing violence as an outcome of a social context that permits or encourages violence. Her analysis is a challenging one for service providers who in her view must educate GLBT communities about the public nature of domestic violence in order to lessen self-blame and encourage connections to additional resources outside of counseling.

Feminist counselors have always held the view that domestic violence is not an individual or couple problem but rather an outcome of a social context that supports misogyny and patriarchy (NiCarthy, 1982; Walker, 1979; Yllo, 1993). Therefore the work of feminist counselors is to help clients see relationship violence as something that is systemic and rooted in gender differences that are based on unequal social power. Yet this gender-based explanation of domestic violence is clearly inappropriate for explaining lesbian partner violence. In this model the lesbian perpetrator may have to be seen as male-like in order for the analysis to fit. For this reason some researchers have rejected feminist approaches and argue instead for a social psychological model that includes an analysis of social oppression but is not gender-based (Hamberger, 1994; Merrill, 1996; Zemsky, 1990). This perspective focuses more on abusive behaviors in relationships, thereby equating heterosexual, gay, lesbian and bisexual relationships while still acknowledging social oppression as a factor.

In my view we cannot simply equate and generalize about all intimate relationships with one totalizing theory, nor can we rely on heterosexual gender-based frameworks for explaining abusive same-sex relationships (Ristock, 1997; Ristock, in press). We need to acknowledge both the similarities and differences between heterosexual domestic violence and lesbian domestic violence without using heterosexuality as the norm through which to understand same-sex relationship dynamics. Given these challenges the question arises as to how feminist counselors currently understand and respond to the issue of abuse in lesbian relationships. Many feminists are providing services specifically for lesbian partner abuse. Among the adjustments they are making to established models of practice designed for heterosexual domestic violence are practices such as couple assessment (determining who is abusing whom in the absence of a clear gender power differential), running support groups for lesbians who have been abused, and creating services for lesbian batterers (Cayouette, 1999; Goddard & Hardy, 1999; Istar, 1996). To date, however, no studies have explored the experiences of feminist service providers in doing this work. This paper reports on a qualitative study that was designed to examine their experiences and in particular how feminist domestic violence theory frames and shapes their responses.

METHOD

This paper is based on eight focus group discussions that were held with seventy feminist counselors in six different Canadian cities (Winnipeg, Manitoba; Vancouver, British Columbia; Calgary, Alberta; Toronto, Ontario; London, Ontario; and Halifax, Nova Scotia). Participants were recruited by contacting domestic violence and GLBT organizations in each city for names of feminist service providers who had a reputation for doing work in this area. Telephone interviews were then conducted with potential participants to tell them about the research and to invite their participation. This study is part of a larger qualitative research project on lesbian partner violence that includes interviews with over 100 women who have experienced abuse in a lesbian relationship (see Ristock, 1998 and Ristock, in press for a description of the larger project and for more details on the methodology).

Focus groups are being used more and more in feminist psychological studies (Montell, 1999; Wilkinson, 1999) because they offer social contexts for meaning-making and involve "collective consciousness work" (Fine, 1992) to be undertaken by participants rather than simply gathering data from them. They also allow for discourse analysis which is useful for seeing the ways that language practices limit and shape our understandings (Burman, 1998; Gavey, 1989; Marecek, 1999; Wilkinson & Kitzinger, 1995). I facilitated each focus group discussion through a dual process of affirmation and disruption (Ristock & Pennell, 1996): I asked questions where we could gather information on the different forms of abuse, power dynamics, and patterns that counselors had noticed and thereby affirm the experiences of lesbians; and I raised issues that disrupted heterosexist assumptions we might hold to explain or account for this form of violence. The framework of discussion questions included items that have been debated within feminist and lesbian communities such as how they defined violence, whether they had ever seen examples of the contested category of "mutual abuse" or shifting power dynamics, whether they considered consensual sadomasochistic relationships as abusive. Participants added to these questions, and discussions lasted 3 to 3 1/2 hours. I served as both a researcher/facilitator and a participant since I could share information from my larger research project as well as share my experiences as a lesbian, as a feminist who has worked in the anti-violence movement, and as someone who has facilitated support groups for abused lesbians.

Participants

The focus group participants ranged in age from 20-63. The majority have a university degree. More than half of the participants identified as lesbian, with a third identifying as heterosexual and a few as bisexual. The participants were, like me, mainly white and included women of color who identified as Native Indian, South Asian, Asian, and Black. Many of the participants worked in agencies including shelters, battered women's services, GLBT organizations, family services, sexual assault centers, women's centers and community resource centers, drug and alcohol addiction programs and university/college counseling services, while some of the participants worked solely as counselors in private practice. They bring a range of experience in the area of domestic violence (1-26 years). They have worked more with heterosexual domestic violence clients than lesbians, and they have seen far fewer gay men.

Analysis

Each focus group was tape-recorded and then transcribed by a research assistant who also attended the discussion. I read over each transcript three or four times to identify themes and discourses. I use discourse analysis to see how meanings are made by paying attention to language and the details of focus group conversations (see Ristock, 1998 for a more complete description of my feminist materialist, discursive, reflexive approach). In this paper I pay attention to both dominant feminist discourses–those that feminists tend to give the status of truth; and marginal feminist discourses–those that challenge certain feminist thinking (Marecek, 1999). In focusing on the dominant and marginal discourses and the spaces in between (contradictions, areas of tension) my analysis reveals the difficulties in bringing forward complexities or counter-discourses in our understandings about lesbian partner violence. They illustrate how we rely on white, feminist heteronormative categories and constructs to think about violence, and ultimately show how these can impede our efforts to respond effectively to same-sex partner abuse. There are many assumptions of normalcy that are at play and that circulate in the discussions. Normative frameworks exist about violence–about victims and perpetrators, about lesbians, and about feminism. Feminist counselors in this study are struggling not simply to see lesbian abuse based on heterosexual understandings–in fact most of the women doing this work are themselves lesbians; but the tendency is to go back to certain standards of normalcy, certain dominant understandings that have been part of feminist theories to explain heterosexual domestic violence. In this paper I present two normative discourses–what Jeanne Marecek (1999) calls "trauma talk" and what I call "necessary speech"–which reflect our struggles and even our inabilities to speak about those aspects of lesbian partner violence that do not fit dominant feminist understandings of relationship violence.

FOCUS GROUP DISCUSSIONS

Dominant Feminist Discourses

Excerpts from focus group discussions are presented to illustrate the normative discourses that I have identified. (See Ristock, in press, where I discuss trauma talk and necessary speech in the context of assessing power dynamics, organizational mandates and running support groups.) The first example arises from a discussion about the similarities and differences between heterosexual abuse and lesbian abuse. It is clear that participants are identifying differences between lesbian and heterosexual abuse. What is also evident is that participants are often uncomfortable with discussions that explore or speculate further on differences that go against dominant feminist thinking in the area of domestic violence. For example:

> BP: I don't know if this is a good question or not, but I'm wondering if there is more insecurity in a lesbian relationship where one partner may have been in a heterosexual relationship before and their partner fears that they'll go back to a heterosexual relationship? I am just wondering whether insecurity could have something to do with abuse, patterns of abuse.

> WW: I myself, I have stayed away from analysis in terms of "stress causes abuse."

> MN: Though it does kind of add to that emotional pressure cooker sort of sense in the relationship. So if there is a propensity to handle problems in a physical way, it [stress] may help to release, to disinhibit that kind of response. (Pause) And I hate myself when I talk like this because I feel really strongly when I talk about perpetrators being held responsible for their behaviors. I work with tons of survivors who've been through hideously abusive experiences. Uh, I have to do some deep breathing around it because [laughter] I think it takes the onus of responsibility off the perpetrator and that really bothers me. So having said what I said, I take it back.

> (Focus Group # 8)

The participant took back what she said because it threatened dominant feminist concepts in which we are deeply invested for good reason: views that see perpetrators as making choices to be violent and never see stress as an explanatory causal factor. The exploratory conversation that was to examine different contexts and dynamics surrounding lesbian abuse was quickly recuperated into a known and accepted normative framework where perpetrators must be held responsible and where details like lesbian partnerships perhaps being more vulnerable because they are not supported by heterosexist institutions and assumptions can remain underanalyzed. As a result, a homogenizing "trauma talk" discourse often became the authoritative and overriding sentiment in focus group discussions about the similarities and differences that allowed people to stay with a focus on the similarities of the effects of violence rather than work further to uncover and address the complexities and differences. The tendency in feminist therapy is to focus our efforts on the results of domestic violence and to assume that we know all we need to know about the causes. Marecek (1999) has identified this discourse in her interview research with feminist therapists. She defines "trauma talk" as a lexicon (a system of terms, metaphors, narrative frameworks) that circulates amongst feminists and others to talk about the physical and sexual abuse of women. Her interest in the trauma talk discourse is to show how therapists' language practices construct clinical realities. For some feminist therapists in her study, the trauma model has become the "sine qua non of feminism in therapy . . . retelling a woman's life as a trauma narrative was both the feminist way and the one true way to tell a life. Yet even though a woman has experienced abuse, narrating her life in terms of that experience produces only one of many possible stories" (p. 170-171). Her comments are relevant for explaining the limits of "trauma talk" in the discussion of lesbian abuse. In focusing only on the violence and in staying with universalist feminist assumptions of what motivates the perpetrator we can erase and ignore any dissonance between heterosexual domestic violence theory and lesbians' experience of domestic violence, and continue with our current thinking and practices.

In another example, participants in each focus group spoke about the concept of mutual abuse and some of the difficulties they have in defining abuse when examining different dynamics they had encountered. Again we see an acknowledgment of differences in lesbian relationship dynamics based on what they have actually heard from clients; yet the tendency is to go back to a known framework rather than make room for new and different experiences. Consider the following example:

> HY: I do think there is something called "mutual abuse," but I don't call it "mutual abuse"; I call it "bad fighting"–"bad dynamics," "power struggles"–I see it as fairly equal in terms of people being in trouble, feeling pretty powerless, pretty helpless, not knowing how to get out of that kind of recursive cycle. Where I don't think it is mutual abuse is where the other person starts hitting back, even if it is not in self-protection, even if the hitting back is out of exhaustion, I don't see that as mutual. I see those actions as speaking more to the impact of abuse and the person [victim] has been so worn out that that's what they do. In the first example they don't talk about the impact in the same way; they were not afraid; they were not exhausted; they were not immobilized in their lives; they were

not isolated from their friends; to me that's a difference [between bad fighting and abuse].

OM: I'm still pondering the question, have I seen mutual abuse and whatever that means? I think about somebody who controls all the money and at the same time the other person is extremely controlling and jealous. And the one who controls the money is very homophobic and doesn't want anyone to know they are lesbians so wants to keep them isolated–is that mutual abuse?

KR: Where I find the language frightening is that working in a shelter with male violence, there are a lot of people in the population who would like to say "Hey this happens to everyone," so they can just defuse it. So I don't want to talk about this and that's why. I don't want to lose the funding, lose the momentum.

(Focus Group # 4)

In this example we can see the force of very real contexts like needing funds to keep shelters operating and the fear that the scale of male violence against women will be underestimated if we talk about woman-to-woman abuse. This is the context within which feminist service providers are working. Often we rely on dominant discourses for solid strategic reasons but this reliance shuts down or limits the thinking and theorizing that we need in this area. I call this tendency a reliance on "necessary speech," that is, speech that invokes the realities of the conditions within which feminists work; in this case, the need for funding and the context of a backlash against feminism. Necessary speech is what is necessary to state so as to reassert the dominant understandings that provide strong explanatory power for the extent of male violence against women. Both "necessary speech" and the "trauma talk" lexicon mentioned earlier have the unintended effect of constructing and affirming heteronormative frameworks to understand lesbian abuse. In this example, the reassertion of dominant feminist understandings limited the possibility of exploring certain distinctions in power dynamics that might well be important in same-sex relationships (possibly equal physical size, shared gender status) that make fighting back more feasible than in heterosexual relationships.

Marginal Feminist Discourses

Focus groups discussions did reveal moments where people were working against normative frameworks rather than recuperating them. This was most evident in discussions about race and sadomasochism where counter-discourses about naming whiteness and acknowledging the possibility of consensual domination were able to emerge.

Naming Whiteness

> JW: Something I want to–it's going off topic a bit–but I want to get a sense of the women that other people work with because I know for me, my experience is primarily working with not a racially diverse group of women–primarily white women maybe a small number of First Nations women. So I want to know who it is that we are talking about, who it is we are basing our experience on?

> It's a struggle and something that needs to be addressed that the women who come forward for services are usually not women of color and it's happening for particular reasons. I want that to be on the table when we are talking about whoever, our experiences are coming from which groups of women?

> [Many voices commenting supportively, but with tension]

> People began reporting on how many women of color they have worked with and what they have done in their practices to address diversity.

> (Focus Group # 6)

A challenge was made to the group to resist centering lesbian relationships based on white, middle-class experiences and although there was tension in the room when the issue was raised, no efforts were made to stop the conversation or change the direction to recuperate a white normative approach. In this example, whiteness became named and marked as a category that demands scrutiny in order to disrupt its unspoken embodiment as truth, normality and trustworthiness. Similarly in all of the focus groups we had discussions about naming and defining violence in cases where there are power complexities; for example, in interracial relationships, in relationships where there are class differences between the partners, and/or differences in physical abilities. Feminist counselors spoke of the limitations of binary assumptions in feminist domestic violence theories that assume all power rests with one person (the perpetrator) which is used against the powerless (the victim). This is evidence of counter-hegemonic discourses being able to be spoken. It shows there is an opening to the challenge for a feminist analysis of lesbian partner abuse to be able to address the interface of sexism, racism, violence and homophobia (Kanuha, 1990; Renzetti, 1998).

Similarly discussions on sadomasochism revealed attempts to disrupt certain dominant feminist homogenizing views. There have been many debates within feminist and lesbian communities about how to understand sadomasochism with some arguing that it is consensual, while others argue it is impossible for women to truly consent in a patriarchy, and still others stating that it is an empowering way to take control and heal from experiences of sexual abuse. These issues all resurfaced when discussing the therapeutic responses of feminist counselors to s/m. In each focus group most of the participants were open to seeing the complexities of women's sexual practices and experiences of abuse rather than forcing a dominant feminist ideological stance. For example:

Consensual S/M

> AM: I did see s/m practices as being abusive and then I changed my position as I learned more, found more out, gained more experience in the whole area . . . yet on a much broader level I still have a problem with it. Yet when I'm working with people I have to be very open so that we can work through different layers so that I don't totally lose them or alienate them.

> GF: How do we learn about the complexities? I think for, myself, I think about my own ignorance about s/m, I'm not part of the s/m community and so I've needed to learn about different practices. I think when it gets difficult is when young women are learning about s/m and who they learn from and in what context and if there has been power imbalances in the relationship already and if you are just coming out and you are coming into s/m, who is teaching you about it? Is it in a context of an already abusive relationship or is it in a safe relationship?

> AM: Those are really important questions.

> [group voices–hmm hmm]

> (Focus Group # 3)

The movement of this discussion shows efforts made by some of the participants to encourage reflexive stances (like asking questions about the context of a relationship, being aware of your own limited knowledge) rather than asserting any either/or positions about the nature of s/m and its relation to abuse. In many of the focus groups s/m was identified as an issue that young queer women want to talk about–for example in four of the six cities where focus groups were conducted the participants mentioned that workshops have been held for GLBT youth groups on this topic, at their request. Most feminist counselors saw their role as needing to get information and being able to create an environment where clients can talk about marginalized sexual practices without being judged. On this issue there was more willingness to move beyond the usual polarization that exists between s/m feminists and anti-s/m domestic violence activists. Participants acknowledged s/m as a sexual practice, thereby resisting dominant feminist domestic violence theory that s/m equals abuse (Margulies, 1999). With this counter discourse they could discuss the ways that some s/m relationships can be abusive while others can be consensual and non-abusive. Counter-discourses in both of these examples (race and s/m) create the possibility of moving away from homogenizing domestic violence in abstract terms to address the specificity and multiplicity of women's lives.

I have provided a few examples from focus groups discussions with feminist counselors on lesbian partner abuse. The discussions that I held reveal the normative discourses that feminist service providers both employ and at times struggle against. The conversations reveal the investments we have in maintaining dominant feminist discourses about relationship violence. In this research feminist counselors often resist counter-discourses and continue to insist on "trauma talk" and "necessary speech." Yet calling attention to language practices shows how the investments in dominant feminist discourses construct and shape reality in ways that are not helpful to women's lives–in fact such investment often went against the very experiences of lesbians that counselors had been witness to.

I also want to comment further on the areas where counter-discourses were able to emerge. Within academic and community feminisms there has been considerable anti-normative discussion over the last twenty years about diversity and the need to move beyond white middle-class women's experiences, and there have been many debates about sadomasochism (although corresponding changes in practice have not always resulted from these challenges). On the other hand, dominant feminist discourses remained in place during focus group discussions about the causes of violence, mutual abuse, and differing power dynamics, areas where we have had far fewer exploratory discussions because of the fear of fueling a backlash against feminism by those theorists and groups who claim that feminists have created a "wife abuse industry" that victimizes innocent men and protects abusive women.

CONCLUSION

Overall, this research suggests that we need more spaces and a language to talk about lesbian relationships and lesbian abuse that move us beyond white, heteronormative frameworks if we are to develop truly inclusive services and appropriate therapeutic practices. For feminist counselors, participating in a focus group was often a welcome opportunity to speak with other counselors about the work they were doing, the dilemmas that they encountered, and the implications for therapeutic practice. Many commented that they are isolated in private practice or isolated within mainstream agencies. Creating more opportunities for discussion will allow us to share new information about same-sex domestic violence and engage in a reflexive process where we can challenge our assumptions and investments in certain positions. Feminist counselors in these focus groups do wish to develop effective responses and interventions in this area. They spoke of the lack of services for perpetrators, the barriers that exist for lesbians of color and the fact that woman-to-woman abuse challenges long cherished ideals about women's relationships with other women. But the conversations were just a beginning step in "collective consciousness work" with some areas opening up and others shutting down. In my view, we can expand a feminist analysis of relationship violence so that we continue to recognize and prevent male violence against women while also broadening our feminist understandings of other forms of interpersonal violence. We need to struggle constantly to find ways of working with women in the local, specific, and contextual while de-centering heterosexuality and resisting even our own normative tendencies.

REFERENCES

Burman, E. (Ed.). (1998). *Deconstructing feminist psychology.* London: Sage Publications.

Cayouette, S. (1999). Running batterers groups for lesbians. In B. Leventhal & S. Lundy (Eds.), *Same-sex domestic violence: Strategies for change* (pp. 233-243). Thousand Oaks, CA: Sage.

Fine, M. (1992). *Disruptive voices: The possibilities of feminist research.* Ann Arbor, MI: University of Michigan Press.

Gavey, N. (1989). Feminist poststructuralism and discourse analysis: Contributions to feminist psychology. *Psychology of Women Quarterly, 13*, 459-475.

Goddard, A.B. & Hardy, T. (1999). Assessing the lesbian victim. In B. Leventhal & S. Lundy (Eds.), *Same-sex domestic violence: Strategies for change* (pp. 193-200). Thousand Oaks, CA: Sage.

Hamberger, L.K. (1994). Domestic partner abuse: Expanding paradigms for understanding and intervention. *Violence and Victims, 9*(2), 91-94.

Istar, A. (1996). Couple assessment: Identifying and intervening in domestic violence in lesbian relationships. In C. Renzetti & C.H. Miley (Eds.), *Violence in gay and lesbian domestic partnerships* (pp. 93-106). New York: Harrington Park Press.

Kanuha, V. (1990). Compounding the triple jeopardy: Battering in lesbian of color relationships. *Women & Therapy 9*, 169-184.

Leventhal, B. & Lundy S.E. (Eds.) (1999). *Same-sex domestic violence: Strategies for change*. Thousand Oaks, CA: Sage.

Lobel, K. (Ed.) (1986). *Naming the violence: Speaking out about lesbian battering*. Seattle, WA: Seal Press.

Marecek, J. (1999). Trauma talk in feminist clinical practice. In S. Lamb (Ed.), *New versions of victims: Feminists struggle with the concept* (pp. 158-182). New York: New York University Press.

Margulies, J. (1999). Coalition building 'til it hurts: Creating safety around s/m and battering. In B. Leventhal & S.E. Lundy (Eds.), *Same-sex domestic violence: Strategies for change* (pp. 135-145). Thousand Oaks, CA: Sage.

Merrill, G. (1996). "Ruling the exceptions: Same-sex battering and domestic violence theory." In C. Renzetti & C.H. Miley (Eds.), *Violence in gay and lesbian domestic partnerships* (pp. 9-22). New York: Harrington Park Press.

Montell, F. (1999). Focus group interviews: A new feminist method. *National Women's Studies Association Journal, 11*(1), 44-69.

NiCarthy, G. (1982). *Getting free: A handbook for women in abusive relationships*. Seattle, WA: Seal Press.

Renzetti, C.M. (1992). *Violent betrayal: Partner abuse in lesbian relationships*. Newbury Park, CA: Sage Publications.

Renzetti, C.M. (1998). Violence and abuse in lesbian relationships: Theoretical and empirical issues. In R.K. Bergen (Ed.), *Issues in intimate violence* (pp. 117-128). Thousand Oaks, CA: Sage Publications.

Renzetti, C. & Miley, C.H. (Eds.) (1996). *Violence in gay and lesbian domestic partnerships*. New York: Harrington Park Press.

Ristock, J. L. (1994). "And justice for all?" . . . The social context of legal responses to abuse in lesbian relationships. *Canadian Journal of Women and the Law, 7,* 415-430.

Ristock, J.L. (1997). The cultural politics of abuse in lesbian relationships: Challenges for community action. In N.V. Benokraitis (Ed.), *Subtle sexism: Current practice and prospects for change* (pp. 279-296). Thousand Oaks, CA: Sage.

Ristock, J.L. (1998). Community-based research: Lesbian abuse and other telling tales. In J.L. Ristock & C.G. Taylor (Eds.), *Inside the academy and out: Lesbian/gay/queer studies and social action* (pp. 137-154). Toronto, ON: University of Toronto Press.

Ristock, J.L. (in press). Exploring dynamics of abusive lesbian relationships: Preliminary analysis of a multi-site, qualitative study. *American Journal of Community Psychology*.

Ristock, J.L. & Pennell, J. (1996). *Community research as empowerment: Feminist links, postmodern interruptions*. Toronto, ON: Oxford University Press.

Russo, A. (1999). Lesbian organizing against lesbian battering. In B. Leventhal & S.E. (Eds.), *Same-sex domestic violence: Strategies for change*, (pp. 83-96). Thousand Oaks, CA: Sage.

Scherzer, T. (1998). Domestic violence in lesbian relationships: Findings of the lesbian relationships research project. *Journal of Lesbian Studies, 2*(1), 29-47.

Turell, S.C. (1999). Seeking help for same-sex relationship abuses. *Journal of Gay & Lesbian Social Services, 10*(2), 35-49.

Walker, L.E. (1979). *The battered woman.* New York: Harper and Row.

Wilkinson, S. (1999). *Focus groups: A feminist method. Psychology of Women Quarterly, 23,* 221-244.

Yllo, K. (1993). Through a feminist lens: Gender, power and violence. In R. Gelles & D. Loseke (Eds.), *Current controversies in family violence.* Newbury Park, CA: Sage Publications.

Zemsky, B. (1990). Lesbian battering; Considerations for intervention. In P. Elliot (Ed.), *Confronting lesbian battering: A manual for the battered women's movement* (pp. 64-67). St. Paul, MN: Minnesota Coalition for Battered Women.

The Power of Shame:
Lesbian Battering
as a Manifestation of Homophobia

Leanne M. Tigert

SUMMARY. The reality of lesbian partner violence has been long un-der-recognized and misunderstood. Treatment protocols based solely upon work with heterosexual batterers and victims are inadequate when working with lesbians. In fact, without recognizing the specific needs of lesbians, treatment may compound rather than cure the problem. This ar-ticle explores lesbian battering as a response to and reenactment of cul-tural oppression, internalized homophobia, and religious/psychological shame. The cycle of domestic violence can be the acting out of the traumatization of homophobia/heterosexism, compounded by sexual and religious shaming. A theology of liberation and the psychology of healing from trauma are explored as critical ingredients to treating vic-tims and perpetrators. *[Article copies available for a fee from The Haworth Document Delivery Service: 1-800-342-9678. E-mail address: <getinfo@ haworthpressinc.com> Website: <http://www.HaworthPress.com> © 2001 by The Haworth Press, Inc. All rights reserved.]*

KEYWORDS. Traumatization of homophobia/heterosexism, reli-gious/sexual shame in lesbian battering

---

Leanne M. Tigert is a licensed pastoral counselor and anti-homophobia educator, author of two books and several articles on homophobia and the psychology of reli-gion, and editor of a forthcoming book by l/g/b/t youth.

Address correspondence to: Leanne M. Tigert, DMin, Womankind Counseling Center, 21 Green Street, Concord, NH 03301 (E-mail: RvLTigert@aol.com).

[Haworth co-indexing entry note]: "The Power of Shame: Lesbian Battering as a Manifestation of Homo-phobia." Tigert, Leanne M. Co-published simultaneously in *Women & Therapy* (The Haworth Press, Inc.) Vol. 23, No. 3, 2001, pp. 73-85; and: *Intimate Betrayal: Domestic Violence in Lesbian Relationships* (ed: Ellyn Kaschak) The Haworth Press, Inc., 2001, pp. 73-85. Single or multiple copies of this article are available for a fee from The Haworth Document Delivery Service [1-800-342-9678, 9:00 a.m. - 5:00 p.m. (EST). E-mail address: getinfo@haworthpressinc.com].

73

She left this time, and is staying with some friends of ours. They are the only people we're out to, and now they know how mean I've been to her. I wanted to get help before it got to this, but nobody knows–about my sexual orientation or my temper.

(thirty year old, Caucasian, closeted lesbian, computer technician)

I feel terrible about it, but, it's like I'm angry all the time. Then she does something that puts me over the edge, and I'm gone. I explode all over her, sometimes with my words, sometimes with my fists. Then we both feel worse.

(twenty-three year old, Latina, lesbian,
alienated from her fundamentalist Christian family of origin)

Everyone thinks we are the model couple–lesbians with kids, a home, we even have a white picket fence! But I'm getting really scared, and it's embarrassing to be afraid of another woman. Mostly she yells. She's only hit me a few times, but the last time it was in front of our kids. She's always sorry and says she won't do it again, but I don't want my kids to grow up like this.

(forty-two year old, Caucasian, openly lesbian nurse,
nonbiological mother of two children)

I tried to talk with my last therapist about this, but I swear, she didn't believe me. It was like she never considered the possibility that a woman could be violent. She told me I was overreacting. Then, she started quizzing me on why I thought I was bisexual!

(thirty-seven year old, Caucasian bisexual woman)

Each of these comments is an example of the dilemmas that lesbian batterers and victims have described in my office over the years. Had they been the experiences of heterosexual couples, I might have been saddened and angered by the realities of domestic violence; however, I would also be able to turn to a readily available protocol of treatment, legal process, and victim support. However, they are not heterosexual couples. Simply to transpose the same regimen of treatment from straight couples and individuals to lesbian couples and individuals is not only counterproductive, but could add to the problem, reinforcing abusive patterns.

Domestic violence is defined as ". . . a pattern of coercive behavior that is used by one person to gain power and control over another, which may include physical violence, sexual, emotional, and psychological intimidation, verbal abuse, stalking, and economic control" (New Hampshire Coalition Against Domestic Violence, 1999). Certainly, this definition is valid, regardless of one's gender or sexual orientation. Nonetheless, lesbian domestic violence is not the same as heterosexual domestic violence. Lesbian partner violence is not only about power and control within an intimate relationship. It is also about homophobia/heterosexism, and the reenactment of and response to cultural traumatization. It is, as Mistinguette Smith Malone, a cultural educator, has said, a form of "oppression sickness," culturally, emotionally, and spiritually (1997). If this "oppression sickness" remains unacknowledged and untreated, then the violence will continue, in one form or another.

The term "homophobia" was initially coined by Dr. George Weinberg in 1972. He begins his book, *Society and the Healthy Homosexual*, by stating that he "would never consider a patient healthy unless he [or she] had overcome . . . prejudice against homosexuality." Weinberg defines homophobia as "the dread of being in close quarters with homosexuals–and in the case of homosexuals themselves, self-loathing" (Weinberg, 1972, pp.1, 4). Heterosexism is the systematizing of homophobic beliefs and assumptions. It provides the structures by which homophobia is held in place. Blumenfeld and Raymond describe it as ". . . so pervasive, heterosexism is hard to detect . . . Heterosexism forces lesbians, gays, and bisexuals to struggle constantly against their own invisibility . . . Heterosexism is discrimination by neglect, omission, and/or distortion . . ." (Blumenfeld and Raymond, 1989, p. 226). Homophobia and heterosexism support the functions of discrimination in society. Specifically, they maintain the economic control and power of the dominant group (white, straight, male), and reinforce the assumption that the traditional family unit, headed by the husband/father/breadwinner is the only acceptable economic structure or unit.

According to Suzanne Pharr (1988), there are common elements in all forms of discrimination, including homophobia. The first element is that of the establishment of a defined norm or standard of rightness. Maintaining this "rightness" requires the use of violence and the threat of violence. Secondly, discrimination asserts that those who fall outside the norm are defined as "the other." This otherness is maintained through invisibility, distortion, and stereotyping, leading toward complicity in one's own oppression. The third element that Pharr describes is internalized oppression, similar to "oppression sickness" which can result in self-hatred, depression, self-abuse, and horizontal hostility.

I recently experienced these elements of discrimination, homophobia, and heterosexism during a phone call with a colleague. A counselor within the prison system, she called to ask if I knew of any services in the area for lesbian batterers. "First of all," she said, "no one seems to want to address the concerns of lesbians in prison. But even before that, in the court system no one seems to believe that lesbian battering even exists. So, instead of alternative treatment programs like straight men have, these women just go to prison to serve time." In this brief conversation, one can see the attitudes of homophobia concretized into the structures of heterosexism, serving the purposes of discrimination.

The term, "trauma" is one of those words which conjures up many different images for people, including treatment providers and recipients. Judith Herman, MD (1992), who has worked with survivors of many types of trauma, defines psychological trauma as " . . . an affliction of the powerless. At the moment of trauma, the victim is rendered helpless by overwhelming force . . . Traumatic events overwhelm the ordinary systems of care that give people a sense of control, connection and meaning" (p. 33). In order to be traumatic, an event does not have to be unusual, only overwhelmingly disempowering. Herman goes on:

> Traumatic events are extraordinary, not because they occur rarely, but rather because they overwhelm the ordinary human adaptations to life . . . traumatic events generally involve threats to life or bodily integrity, or a close personal encounter with violence and death. They confront human beings with the extremities of helplessness and terror, and evoke the responses of catastrophe. (p. 33)

Out of my own professional and personal experiences, I could relate hundreds of examples from the lives of lesbian/gay/bisexual/transgender people which substantiate this definition of trauma. Queer people understand the ordinariness of trauma all too well. It is a never-ceasing trauma, or traumatization, to be consistently rendered one-down, second-class, disempowered, and less safe just because of who we are and whom we love. I know this every time my partner and I walk down the street holding hands. Some portion of my psyche is doing 360 degree turns checking all the streets and alleys, just in case we need to be ready for a violent reaction from someone.

It is my belief that gay/lesbian/bisexual/trangender people in our society experience degrees of ongoing traumatization from the very beginning of our lives. Oppression yields trauma. Consciously and/or unconsciously, we know that the world is not safe for us, as it is similarly unsafe for people of color, women, differently-abled persons, low-income people, and all who challenge the power and privilege of the white, heterosexual, able-bodied, Christian, and wealthy male. Although the experience of oppression varies, there are some commonalities of traumatization which we share. Each of us, unless we live in a state of constant denial, knows on some level that we could be victimized by someone's nonrational rage at any moment. Bessel A. Van der Kolk (1996), another leading expert in the diagnosis and treatment of traumatic stress, raises many significant points about trauma and its effects. Van der Kolk says that the traumatic event itself is not primary in one's recovery, but that the meaning of the event is key.

> ... the critical element that makes an event traumatic is the subjective assessment by victims of how threatened and helpless they feel . . . the meaning that victims attach to these events is as fundamental as the trauma itself . . . For many patients, what is most destructive about a traumatic event is that it confirms some long-feared belief, rather than presenting them with a novel incongruity. (pp. 6-8)

In a recent article in *The Advocate,* a well-known national gay and lesbian newsmagazine, several violent anti-gay/lesbian hate crimes were reported to be the result of self-hate projected onto the victim, with the leading question "Are bashers killing the gay part of themselves when they attack gay men?" (Dahir, 2000). In a similar manner, I believe that much same-sex domestic and sexual violence stems from the internalization of homophobia and the lack of tools to cope effectively with cultural trauma. Ongoing systemic homophobia becomes traumatic because it confirms the belief that lesbians (and gay men) are appropriate objects of violence and hatred. In this society we learn that it is okay to take verbal and physical hits at non-heterosexuals. In some sense, lesbian batterers, like gay-bashers, are acting out society's prescription for behavior. This in no way means that lesbians who batter are not responsible for their actions. It only means they could be treated more effectively.

Several years ago, a lesbian non-biological mother of two children called for a therapy appointment. Her initial concern was that she had broken up with her partner, had no legal ties to her children, and was told by their biological mother that she would not be allowed contact. My client was very closeted, and felt overwhelmed by the "outting" that would happen if she went to court to seek legal visitation. In addition, she had very few skills of self-reflection, tending to blame her partner for all the family problems. She appeared highly agitated and vigilant, and described herself as "having a problem with anger." Eventually, she told me that she would often throw things in the house when she was mad at her partner, sometimes yelling and calling her demeaning names. She finally admitted to hitting her once. She also told me that her father used to be very controlling, and a few times hit her mother to "keep her in line." She described that when she came out to her family of origin her father "went beserk," screaming that she was "sick and perverted," and threw a coffee cup across the kitchen. She wonders if he is right–"Maybe I am sick. Maybe being gay is wrong. I hate my father, but I'm acting just like him. What's wrong with me?"

Obviously, trying to treat this woman's abusive behaviors without understanding the traumatizing role of homophobia and heterosexism in her life would be ineffective. She must learn to negotiate the legal, social, religious, and familial structures of heterosexism, and her own internalized homophobia and shame before she will be able to participate in a healthy, violence-free relationship.

Lesbian/gay/bisexual/transgender folk do not go through the process of creating a healthy sexual identity within a vacuum. We bring our own histories, needs, scars, strengths, and gifts to the process. Lesbians who are raised within a culture of sexism and homophobia must un-learn these lessons in order to be healthy. Lesbians who are raised in violent and abusive households may learn violent and abusive behaviors. Many studies of family violence show a high correlation between the tendency to abuse others and one's own history of witnessing and/or being abused. But while some victims become abusers, many others become protectors of others from abuse. Still others continue to face life from the stance and perspective of a victim for many years. Often in couples, whether opposite or same-gender, one person takes out anger that belongs elsewhere on their partner. When working with lesbians, it is important to name anger as a possible manifestation of homophobia. Lesbians, as is the case with all victims of discrimination, must address what we have internalized so that we do not fall into the trap of victimizing others.

Other studies show that once a person has been victimized, then he or she is more likely than others to be victimized again. In other words, rape victims are more likely to be raped again, and childhood sexual abuse survivors (one out of three females) are more likely to be abused as adults (Russell, 1984). If we are to take the traumatization of homophobia and heterosexist oppression seriously, then we must address the risk of repeated trauma that lesbians live with on a daily basis, because of both our gender and our sexual orientation. Throughout the years of my practice, I have sat with many lesbian women who were sexually or physically victimized as children or young adults, and then re-victimized by controlling and/or abusive women partners as adults. Developing enough ego-strength and moving through shame in order to believe in their own worth and advocate for themselves becomes the major focus of treatment with many of these women.

Often, I have witnessed gay/lesbian/bisexual/transgender people put themselves into situations and relationships in which they know they will be scoffed at, ridiculed, or ignored. Is this type of behavior also an unconscious reenactment of the chronic homophobia with which we live? Perhaps. As might be expected, the more that people come out and seek healing from external and internalized homophobia, the less they tolerate attachments that harm and silence them.

THE ROLE OF SHAME

Closely connected to the impact of internalized homophobia is the emotion of shame. Because our sexuality and sexual orientation are deeply interwoven with and emerge from our core sense of ourselves, to be shamed for one's sexual orientation is to be shamed for one's very self. Thus, one feels "bad" deep within; perhaps unredeemable. Overcoming shame is a key part of the core spiritual and psychological work of overcoming homophobia. Shame is a critical feature in all aspects of violence and victimization as well. However, it is especially significant in the cycle of lesbian battering. Shame is about control, and sexual shame is about sexual control. Sexual shame is often projected onto gay/lesbian/bisexual/transgender folk as a means of social and religious sexual control. Then it is internalized and often acted out by us as the objects of that control. Thus, to overcome sexual shame is to overcome homophobia and vice versa. Shame is at the core of numerous psychological and spiritual concerns–depression, anxiety, addictions, isolation, violence, perfectionism, and spiritual alienation. It is imperative to uncover its potential role in every violent episode in order to create change.

Shame is defined by Merle Fossum and Marilyn Mason (1989) as the following:

> Shame is an inner experience of being completely diminished or insufficient as a person. A moment of shame may be humiliation so painful or an indignity so profound that one feels one has been robbed of her or his dignity or exposed as basically inadequate, bad, or worthy of rejection. A pervasive sense of shame is the ongoing premise that one is fundamentally bad, inadequate, defective, unworthy, or not fully valid as a human being. (p. 31)

In their work on the role of shame in the lives of lesbians and gay men, Kaufman and Raphael (1996) make the connection between shame, difference, and sexual control.

> It is virtually impossible to be different, particularly in this culture, and not feel deficient for the difference . . . First we are devalued by others, and then we devalue ourselves. Because of the close connection between the awareness of difference and shame, being gay or lesbian inescapably

marks us as lesser . . . We become outcast in our own culture . . . To be sick, to be unnatural, to be judged evil–these are beyond question shameful. Being seen as gay or lesbian therefore unavoidably targets anyone for shaming. (p. 7)

Thus, one can see the deep and intertwining connection between the pervasiveness of cultural homophobia/heterosexism and the importance of core sexual shame. Many lesbian and bisexual women must cope with this social shaming under a shroud of silence and isolation. Often, battering occurs when couples are distant and far removed from others, hidden behind a veil of secrecy. The shame of being battered by a woman or of being a woman who batters often prevents these women from getting help.

In his work on shame, D. L. Nathanson (1992) describes four basic defensive reactions to shame. He names these reactions as withdrawal, avoidance, attack the self, and attack the other. Essentially, these form what many people experience as the "flight or fight" syndrome when feeling threatened by danger. I find this to be a very helpful framework in trying to discern the motivations and impact of someone's behaviors. Specifically determining whether an individual habitually responds with one pattern or another can enable him or her to move through the power of shame toward affirmation and healing.

The third and fourth patterns of attacking the self or attacking the other are particularly relevant in the treatment of lesbian batterers and victims. The emotional dynamics between lesbian partners may be so charged that, in fact, the batterer may feel that at some core level, she is attacking herself when she hits her partner. One of the vignettes at the beginning of this article was that of a lesbian batterer who had been alienated from her family of origin due to their fundamentalist religious beliefs. After engaging in a long course of treatment, she was able to name that ". . . every time I hit my partner I was hitting myself. There was too much loss. I was too angry. I always felt horrible afterwards, but some part of me felt we both deserved it."

The fourth pattern of behavior in acting out shame is that of attacking the other. Clearly this action is connected to the experience of being shamed into a feeling of inferiority to others, and is an attempt to feel better about oneself by demoralizing or hurting someone else. This is often a misguided and dangerous attempt to prove one's power and control when she is feeling utterly powerless and out of control. The perceived benefit in this strategy is that it takes the focus off of oneself and places it elsewhere, hence avoiding the painful internal and personal work which must be done. Thus, to question the level of homophobic shame and its acting out should always be addressed when a lesbian is abusive towards her partner.

THE RELIGIOUS ROOTS OF HOMOPHOBIA
AND DOMESTIC VIOLENCE

Trying to help women heal their "oppression sickness" without addressing the religious roots of homophobia and the spiritual sources of recovery often misses the foundation upon which violence and victimhood may be built. Perhaps as many as 90% of the lesbian and bisexual women with whom I work have internalized some degree of spiritual shame–feeling, if not believing, themselves to be bad, immoral, strong, or evil in some eternal manner. Left ignored, this can sabotage any hope for long-lasting healing. After all, if one considers herself and her partner "condemned for all eternity," what really is the point of investing in the work to become violence-free?

> Religious evil occurs whenever the theology and/or practices of religious groups are used to destroy bodies and spirits. Religious evil is the most dangerous kind of evil, because it obscures the possibility of a transcendent reality to which communities of resistance can appeal. (Poling, 1996, xv)

The religious evil of homophobia seeks to destroy the soul of a lesbian, turning her from knowing herself as a sacred being into a sexual object to be scorned. Due to her gender and sexual orientation, she becomes a kind of spiritual scapegoat. Historically, religious scapegoats have been placed in exile, and then destroyed. Many lesbians who act out in violent manners toward themselves and others have experienced this level of spiritual shame at some point in their lives (Tigert, 1999). Kathleen Sands (1994), a feminist theologian in the Boston area, would describe lesbian batterers and victims as persons who act in "spirit-scarring" manners, with limited choices. Specifically, she says that because of the power and presence of evil, people are forced to make choices that in principle might seem wrong, but in practice, are understandable. "But people live in practice, not in principle, and in practice people make spirit-scarring choices every day" (p. 7).

Liberation theology is a vital tool in the dismantling of homophobia and heterosexism. So much of heterosexist thought and practice appeals to Jewish and Christian scripture that even non-church-goers fall back on patriarchal religious dogma to defend the oppression of gay, lesbian, bisexual, and transgender persons. In his book, *Know My Name: A Gay Liberation Theology* (1995), Richard Cleaver describes a four-stage theological process of healing this religious shaming similar to that of Bonganjalo Goba, a leading liberation theologian in South Africa. These steps are particularly helpful to people raised within major religious traditions.

First, Cleaver says, we take our starting point from experience. The circle is set in motion by a question arising out of our experience that does not gel with what we have been taught. This leads to the second stage of suspicion. Our suffering and pain make us suspicious of our inherited teachings, because the teachings do not alleviate any suffering. In fact, they contribute to it. Thirdly, we search the scriptures in new ways, seeking new insights and wrestling with previously unnoticed events, people, messages, and meanings. In the case of gay/lesbian/bisexual/transgender issues, this search may turn up a number of previously overlooked sexual outlaws with radical openness to the word and work of God; and therefore, become the mediators of messengers of God's grace. Finally, we use the newly heard message to interpret the reality that sent us searching in the first place.

What is healing for people spiritually is also healing for us psychologically. Therefore, the steps and characteristics which free people theologically and spiritually, also liberate us psychologically and emotionally. I know this to be true from my experience with women engaged in various stages of the coming out process. Thus, healing the cycle of lesbian battering and violence calls us to work together on many fronts simultaneously.

As pastor and therapist, I have been quite privileged to witness the workings of this spiritual and psychological healing. Repeatedly, as women come out, speak the truth of their lives to others, and learn from one another's struggles and celebrations, they broaden and deepen in mind, soul, and body. Some attach religious meaning and language to this process, while others talk only in terms of emotional and relational well-being. Even so, if spirituality is truly freeing, then it liberates the whole of our being. Likewise, if one experiences a new level of psychological and relational health and well-being, then the spirit is less constricted and increasingly open to the larger life force/Spirit/Higher Power/God/ess.

Over and over and over again, it is becoming clear that the single most important step in recovering from the power of internalized homophobia and violence is the step out of the closet. Specifically, coming out to oneself and to others flies in the face of the conspiracy of silence perpetrated by homophobia and heterosexism. The power of homophobia is like the power of the abuser who says, "Don't tell or I will kill you! Don't tell–they won't believe you; they will make fun of you; they will cut you off; you will be publicly shamed and humiliated! I am right. You are wrong. I am in control. You are the victim, and you have no choice but to victimize yourself or someone else."

> Society force-feeds us the poison of shame, and we grow our own clos-
> ets, develop our own internalized homophobia. Coming out is the only
> antidote, the way to claim, or reclaim, our true selves . . . it frees our

voices, our energies, and ultimately our most creative and empowered selves.... Coming out is always worth it ... Nobody regrets coming out, no matter what the consequences. (Osborne, 1996, p. 24)

My own professional and personal experience affirms the truth of this statement. Thus far, I have yet to hear a client, parishioner, or friend say that she wished she had not come out, even if it meant the loss of relationships, career, or perceived safety. However, we cannot come out in isolation, without true support, valid connections, and adequate information. Research is clear that coming out within an environment of care and counsel creates the kind of positive outcomes which are necessary prerequisites to healing violence. In his research on lesbians and gay men, pastoral theologian, Larry Kent Graham (1997) names and describes "outcomes of positively experienced care." He lists these as:

1. The ability to move from self-hatred to self-esteem,
2. The ability to move from alienation from God to tentative reconciliation,
3. The ability to move from phoniness and dishonesty to truthfulness and genuineness in relationships,
4. The ability to move from self-absorption to self-giving love,
5. The ability to move from vocational malaise to vocational vitality,
6. The ability to move from sexual shame to erotic pleasure. (18-20)

Obviously this kind of change provides a basis from which lesbians might heal their roles and behaviors as victim and perpetrator of violence. One cannot possibly make these kinds of changes and continue behavior that objectifies and harms oneself and/or one's intimate partner.

If these are the outcomes of care, then the tools for healing from trauma provide a framework for the process. For example, Judith Herman describes the process of recovery from trauma as requiring three stages: the establishment of safety, remembrance and mourning, and reconnection with ordinary life. In the work with same-gender domestic violence, these stages form a parallel process. Specifically, one must be safe from physical harm perpetrated by one's partner while, at the same time, she becomes safe from the cultural, religious, and psychological violence of homophobic shame. One must grieve the impact and reality of domestic violence as well as the multiple losses created by homophobia and heterosexism. Finally, one reconnects with violence-free life, and establishes a new connection with an affirming and non-homophobic, respect-based community. Obviously, the work required to heal from trauma is the work required to heal from homophobia and heterosexism.

In sum, the reality of violence within intimate lesbian partnerships may be a result of the acting-out patterns of internalized psychological and spiritual homophobia and shame. Oppression is violent, and violence is traumatizing. People are harmed and then silenced in their pain until positive connections and reconnections are made, and the healing process begun. Yes, there are certain protocols of response to and treatment of domestic violence which must be followed. Similarly, there are dynamics about relational power and control which inform work with same-gender partner abuse. However, without taking into account the harm of homophobia/heterosexism and the realities of cultural oppression, we can never address the source of much of this violence. To address the reality of the homophobic traumatization and its reenactment is to offer understanding, support, knowledge, accountability, community, and hope to women who have been silenced and shamed far too long.

REFERENCES

Blumenfeld, Warren and Raymond, Diane. (1972). *Looking at gay and lesbian life.* New York: St. Martin's Press, 1, 4.

Cleaver, Richard. (1995). *Know my name: A gay liberation theology.* Louisville: Westminster John Knox Press, 11.

Dahir, Mubarak. (2000). "Are bashers killing the gay part of themselves when they attack gay men?" *The Advocate news magazine.* Los Angeles, CA.

Fossum, Merle A. and Mason, Marilyn J. (1989). *Facing shame: Families in recovery.* New York: W.W. Norton, 31.

Graham, Larry Kent. (1997). *Discovering images of God: Narratives of care among lesbians and gays.* Louisville: Westminster John Knox Press, 18-20.

Herman, Judith. (1992). *Trauma and recovery: The aftermath of violence–from domestic abuse to political terror.* New York: Basic Books, 30, 33.

Kaufman, Gershan and Raphael, Lev. (1996). *Coming out of shame: Transforming gay and lesbian lives.* New York: Doubleday, 7.

Nathenson, D.L. (1992). *Shame and pride: Affect, sex, and the birth of the self.* New York: W.W. Norton, 307.

Osborne, Torie. (1996). *Coming home to America: A roadmap to gay and lesbian empowerment.* New York: St. Martin's Press, 24.

Pharr, Suzanne. (1988). *Homophobia: A weapon of sexism.* Little Rock: Chardon Press, 53-64.

Poling, James Nelson. (1996). *Deliver us from evil: Resisting racial and gender oppression.* Minneapolis: Ausburg Fortress Press, xv.

Russell, D.E. (1984). *Sexual exploitation: Rape, child sexual abuse, and sexual harassment.* Beverly Hills, CA: Sage.

Sands, Kathleen. (1994). *Escape from paradise: Evil and tragedy in feminist theology.* Minneapolis: Ausburg Fortress Press, 7.

Smith-Malone, Mistinguette. A speech given at the June 1997 United Church of Christ Coalition for Lesbian, Gay, Bisexual, and Transgender Concerns, Columbus, OH.

Tigert, Leanne McCall. (1996). *Coming out while staying in: Struggles and celebrations of lesbians, gays, and bisexuals in the church.* Cleveland: Pilgrim Press.

Tigert, Leanne McCall. (1999). *Coming out through fire: Surviving the trauma of homophobia.* Cleveland: Pilgrim Press.

Van der Kolk, Bessel A., McFarlane, Alexander C., and Weisaeth, Lars, eds. (1996). *Traumatic stress: The effects of overwhelming experience of mind, body, and society.* New York: Guilford Press, 6-10.

Lesbians Who Abuse Their Partners: Using the FIRO-B to Assess Interpersonal Characteristics

Paula B. Poorman

Sheila M. Seelau

SUMMARY. This study explored the functional, interpersonal style of a small group of lesbians who had abused their partners ($N = 15$) and enrolled in a pilot feminist abuse cessation therapy program. Each completed a Fundamental Interpersonal Relations Orientation-Behavior scale (FIRO-B), a self-report assessment tool that measures expressed and wanted inclusion, control, and affection. Robust findings from the small, ethnically homogenous sample are discussed in terms of their implications for understanding one interpersonal dynamic of control in lesbian relationships in which there is abuse. Future directions for therapy and research are also outlined. *[Article copies available for a fee from The Haworth Document Delivery Service: 1-800-342-9678. E-mail address: <getinfo@haworthpressinc.com> Website: <http://www.HaworthPress.com> © 2001 by The Haworth Press, Inc. All rights reserved.]*

Paula B. Poorman, PhD, is Assistant Professor, Department of Psychology, University of Wisconsin-Whitewater; Sheila M. Seelau, PhD, is Assistant Professor, Department of Psychology, University of Wisconsin-Whitewater.

The authors thank Eric P. Seelau, who advised about the statistical analysis, and those who kindly volunteered to participate in the study.

Address correspondence to: Paula B. Poorman, PhD, Department of Psychology, Winther Hall, 800 West Main Street, Whitewater, WI 53190-1790 (E-mail: poormanp@uwwvax.uww.edu).

[Haworth co-indexing entry note]: "Lesbians Who Abuse Their Partners: Using the FIRO-B to Assess Interpersonal Characteristics." Poorman, Paula B., and Sheila M. Seelau. Co-published simultaneously in *Women & Therapy* (The Haworth Press, Inc.) Vol. 23, No. 3, 2001, pp. 87-105; and: *Intimate Betrayal: Domestic Violence in Lesbian Relationships* (ed: Ellyn Kaschak) The Haworth Press, Inc., 2001, pp. 87-105. Single or multiple copies of this article are available for a fee from The Haworth Document Delivery Service [1-800-342-9678, 9:00 a.m. - 5:00 p.m. (EST). E-mail address: getinfo@haworthpressinc.com].

KEYWORDS. Lesbian, domestic abuse, FIRO-B, control

The fact of same-sex abuse has invited some to break with the original feminist sociopolitical analyses and propose gender-neutral theories that focus on the personality characteristics of batterers (e.g., Dutton, 1998; Island & Letellier, 1991). The last 20 years have seen a proliferation of literature focused on assessing and cataloging types of male batterers. Although this individualistic approach threatens a return to identifying what has been considered political as personal pathology, feminist analysts and individualists actually share an important common tenet. Feminist theories of abuse have been adamant that abuse cannot be and is not the responsibility of the victim/survivor of abuse. If this is so, then it is also clear that both the cause and consequence of woman abuse is the abuser. That said, it is the abuser whose behavior must change to effect a nonviolent relationship. Clearly, understanding the abuser can facilitate this change.

Feminists may depart from the individualists, however, in our recognition that stopping the abusive behavior alone will not effect a violence-free social milieu. Maintaining the changes requires addressing each of the various individual and social forces that serve to support the abuse. The abuser does not exist in a social vacuum and, as feminists (and many new proponents of batterer typology) point out, efforts to change a milieu that has condoned violence against the subordinated, must still involve a multifaceted (Hamberger, 1996; Hamberger & Hastings, 1991) if not an ecological approach (Edleson & Tolman, 1992).

No less than 20 typologies of batterer profiles have been proposed to account for differences among men who abuse women. Comprehensive efforts to review and catalog differences demonstrate that a variety of factors have been included (Holtzworth-Munroe & Stuart, 1994). Early family experiences as witness (e.g., Cadsky & Crawford, 1988; Fagan, Stewart, & Hansen, 1983; Hershorn & Rosenbaum, 1991) or victim (Cadsky & Crawford, 1988; Fagan et al., 1983; Hershorn & Rosenbaum, 1991; Saunders, 1992; Shields, McCall, & Hanneke, 1988), interruptions or deficiencies in attachment that result in dependency and deficiencies in empathy (Cadsky & Crawford, 1988; Caesar, 1986; Elbow, 1977; Faulk, 1974; Hamberger & Hastings, 1985, 1986; Saunders, 1992; Shields et al., 1988; Stith, Jester, & Bird, 1992), and deficiencies in social skills both within and without a primary relationship (Caesar, 1986; Faulk, 1974; Stith et al., 1992) have all been identified as interpersonal dimensions along which abusers vary.

A number of studies have attempted to collapse specific traits into associated personality disorders using measures like the Minnesota Multiphasic Personality Inventory (MMPI) or Millon Clinical Multiaxial Inventory (MCMI; e.g., Caesar & Hamberger, 1989; Hamberger & Hastings, 1986, 1988, 1991; Hastings & Hamberger, 1988). When compared to non-batterers, batterers as a group exhibit characteristics of several personality disorders, including schizoid, borderline, narcissistic, passive dependent and passive aggressive, and compulsive.

Typological studies have identified important interpersonal deficits and pathology prevalent in the clinical samples and, indeed, quantitative evidence suggests that men who fit these profiles seem to constitute a larger proportion of the identified treatment population (Tolman & Bennett, 1990). However, typology research reveals a number of methodological limitations (Holtzworth-Munroe & Stuart, 1994; Tolman & Bennett, 1990). First, with the exception of Stith et al. (1992), who included college students in dating relationships, typology work has focused on clinical populations; and with two exceptions (Allen, Calsyn, Fehrenbach, & Benton, 1989; Barnett & Hamberger, 1992), who used the California Personality Inventory (CPI) and the Fundamental Interpersonal Relations Orientation-Behavior (FIRO-B), typology researchers have used measures designed to assess pathology. The most positive descriptions available comment only on the "absence of clear pathology" (Hamberger & Hastings, 1986). No mention can be made of functional behaviors utilizing tools designed to measure only dysfunction. However, as even the studies themselves point out, woman abuse is not limited to those men (or women) with personality problems, although they may be among the first to volunteer for or be mandated into treatment. Including abusers who reflect a more functional range of variability among broader samples might reflect changeable interpersonal skills deficits rather than immutable personality traits.

Second, Holtzworth-Munroe and Stuart (1994) recommended replication of the often unitary findings to validate further the generalizability of the results and, if the findings presume personality characteristics, to assess stability over time. A third difficulty is the applicability of the massive research protocols used to factor or cluster analyze results. The research instruments have been far too lengthy to be useful in most clinical settings and even cumbersome for many research programs. Fourth, with the recent exception of White and Gondolph (2000), studies have not adequately linked typologies to treatment options. On a more practical note, linking dysfunctional behavior changes to treatment recommendations may be more economically defensible than linking personality disorders to treatment options. The managed care industry generally views the treatment of personality disorders as unprofitable. So, even assuming that specific personality disorders could be eventually linked to abuse, securing treatment for abusers diagnosed with personality disorders will remain more difficult than securing treatment to change specific behaviors.

No research to date has studied typologies including gay or lesbian partners who abuse. This compromises the breadth of our understanding of abuser dynamics. Further, including orientation and gender as dimensions may well hold information critical to integrating feminist and individualist approaches. As Tolman and Bennett point out, typologies are harmful which "cloud the role of social influences or overemphasize spurious differences" (1990, p. 88).

In summary, research has shown that the characteristics of men who batter are highly heterogeneous. Studies themselves evidence the (a) absence of brief assessment tools, (b) absence of examination of "normal," everyday interpersonal functioning, (c) absence of samples based on non-clinical populations, and (d) exclusion of same-sex abusers. The question remains whether identifiable clusters of attributes exist that are relevant to feminist work with lesbians who abuse.

The need for effective change mechanisms for lesbians who abuse is reason enough to argue for an integration of the feminist sociopolitical analysis and the exploration of typologies. If combined with other levels of personality and interpersonal analysis, a brief, effective tool for assessing abusers' functional strengths and limits could link to specific skill development in treatment. If such a tool also explicated rather than obscured the connections between the individual behaviors and important social variables (e.g., the social context in which the behavior occurs; the milieu of unequal power distributions; culturally supported patterns in relationships), such a mechanism could serve research, evaluation, and clinical purposes.

This study explored the functional, interpersonal style of a small group of lesbians who abused their partners and referred themselves for a pilot feminist therapy program designed to hold them accountable for cessation of abuse. The study utilized a brief assessment tool suggested in previous studies because of its emphasis on critical dimensions of interpersonal function thought to be implicated in abuse (Allen et al., 1989; Barnett & Hamberger, 1992). There were five objectives of this study. The first was to identify whether a brief tool, designed to measure everyday interpersonal functioning, would provide meaningful information about the functional interpersonal style of lesbians who abuse. In other words, would mean scores fall within normal limits (< 2 standard deviations from a normative sample) and still provide information critical to understanding lesbians who abused their partners? Second, would lesbians who abuse evidence critical or characteristic similarities and differences from others on interpersonal dimensions? Specifically, we wanted to know where the mean scores of lesbians who abuse would reflect significant similarities or differences from normative samples and from men who abuse.

Third, we wanted to know whether an instrument emphasizing normal everyday interpersonal functioning could evidence sufficient sensitivity to distinguish between lesbians who abused their partners and lesbians who had been abused by their partners. A fourth objective was to identify specific interpersonal skill deficits that could be linked to treatment recommendations. Finally, we hoped to be able to integrate social influences with individual interpersonal profiles by examining interpersonal dynamics relative to dominance and subordination.

METHOD

Participants

Fifteen lesbians (ages 22 to 51; mean age = 32), who had voluntarily enrolled in a therapy group for lesbians who abused their partners, volunteered to participate in this study by authorizing the use of intake and program data. All participants were self-referred to the therapy group. Most heard of the therapy program through general lesbian community sources (80%); two participants heard of the program through the courts (14%); and three heard of the program from their partners (20%).[1]

The majority of the participants were Anglo-American (86.7%), single (60%), and had never been married to men (60%). One woman self-identified as American Indian (6%). Three were divorced from men (20%), and four were living with a lesbian partner or significant other (26%). One participant reported having children who lived with her (6%).

Most participants reported no religious affiliation (47%) or identified religious affiliations other than those listed (26%). Two participants were Catholic (14%), and one was Protestant (6%). Three of the participants identified themselves as having a physical disability (20%).

Most participants had completed some college (mean years of education = 15) and were employed full-time (47%). Five were employed part-time (33%), and three were not employed (20%). Incomes ranged from less than $5,000 a year to well over $40,000 (mean income range = $10,000 to $15,000).

To assess whether their abuse was generalized or confined to intimate partners, participants were asked with whom they had been violent. Nine participants reported violence toward a lesbian partner (60%).[2]
In current or recent relationships, two participants had assault charges pressed against them by their lesbian partners (14%), and one participant had been convicted of assaulting her partner (6%). One participant had obtained a restraining order against her partner for an unspecified offense (6%). Participants also gave numerous reports of abuse in previous relationships. Twelve reported vi-

olence against a lesbian ex-partner (80%), and four reported they had abused a male ex-partner (26%). Four reported abusing a parent (26%), ten reported abusing another family member (67%), and three reported violence against children (20%). Five reported violence toward a friend (33%), and six had been violent toward a stranger or acquaintance (40%).

All participants were asked about their use of prescription and non-prescription drugs. One participant reported taking Tegretol "for depression." Half of the participants reported that at the time of abusive incidents they had been using or abusing chemicals (e.g., alcohol, marijuana, cocaine; 53%). Half also reported that their partners had been using or abusing chemicals during violent incidents (53%).

Comparative group. Twelve lesbians who had been abused by lesbian partners served as a comparative group. These women, who had voluntarily enrolled in a psychoeducational program designed to address their victimization, volunteered to participate in this study by authorizing the use of intake and program data. All women in the comparative group were self-referred to the psychoeducational program. Most heard of the program through general lesbian community sources (67%); one heard of the program through her partner (8%). The comparative group was very similar to the participant group, with no statistically significant differences in their background data (e.g., income, education), except for their reports of abuse and chemical use. Fewer lesbians who had been abused reported that chemicals had been used by them or their partners during violent incidents.

Instrument

The Fundamental Interpersonal Relations Orientation-Behavior (FIRO-B; Schutz, 1978) is a 54-item self-report instrument that measures expressed and wanted inclusion, control, and affection along six separate scale scores. Individuals vary in the degree to which they express these needs or manifest them in their behavior, as well as the degree to which they want each type of interpersonal behavior from others. Expressed inclusion (eI) refers to the need to associate with other people and includes items like "I try to be with people." Expressed control (eC) refers to the extent to which a person assumes responsibility, makes decisions, or dominates people and includes items like "I try to have others do things the way I want them done." Expressed affection (eA) refers to the degree to which a person becomes emotionally involved with others and includes items like "I try to have close personal relationships with others." On the other hand, wanted inclusion (wI) reflects the extent to which a person wants others to include them and is exemplified by items like "I like people to invite me to things." Wanted control (wC) refers to the extent to which the person wants others to make decisions for them and includes items like "I let other people control my actions." Wanted affection (wA) indicates the degree to which someone would like affection to be shown toward them and includes items like "I like people to act close and personal with me." The FIRO-B takes about 20 minutes to administer and about 20 minutes to score.

Responses to each item are made on a six-point scale ranging from "never" to "usually" and are scored based on cut-off points for each item. The number of responses falling above the cut-off for each item are summed, resulting in scores for each scale that range from 0 (low) to 9 (high). Some have debated the influence of social desirability in responses and the validity (Gluck, 1979), but the scales have fairly consistently demonstrated at least adequate reliability and validity in measuring these interpersonal dimensions.

The six FIRO-B scales were derived through Guttman scaling, which suggests reproducibility testing for reliability (Schutz, 1978). Schutz also reported reproducibility coefficients of .94 for all scales except expressed control which was .93. One month test-retest reliability coefficients were .82 for expressed inclusion, .75 for wanted inclusion, .74 for expressed control, .71 for wanted control, .73 for expressed affection, and .80 for wanted affection. Numerous studies have demonstrated the concurrent validity of the FIRO-B scales (e.g., Gluck, 1983; Kramer, 1980).

Procedure

As one part of an extensive intake procedure, participants completed the FIRO-B. Each FIRO-B protocol was scored for eI, eC, eA, wI, wC, and wA. Each protocol received a score that summed expressed and wanted inclusion, control, and affection (ΣI, ΣC, ΣA respectively). Each received a score that reflected the sum of all expressed scales (Σe) and the sum of all wanted scales (Σw). Each received a score that reflected the differences between expressed and wanted inclusion, control, and affection (dI, dC, dA). Finally, each received a score that summed all expressed and wanted inclusion, control, and affection (Σ).

RESULTS

One-sample t tests (SPSS, version 10) compared mean scores on each scale for the lesbians who abused their partners with two normative samples, one group of nurses from the original standardization sample for the FIRO-B (Schutz, 1978) and a group of male batterers (Allen et al., 1989). Using t tests for independent samples, mean scores on each scale were also compared to mean scores of lesbians who had been abused by their partners. Lesbians who were abused by their partners were also compared to the same normative sample of nurses (Schutz, 1978). Alpha was set at < .05 for each of the *t* tests.

Among the original standardization samples for the FIRO-B was an all-female group ($N = 16$) of adult nurses similar in age (range 23 to 55) and educational background (12 to 18 years) to the participants in this sample. The group of adult nurses was the only all-female group among the original standardization samples. In a much larger mixed sample of male and female adult teachers ($N = 677$), teachers' scores were significantly lower than the nurses' scores in both expressed and wanted affection, but in no other scales. Although the normative sample size was small, the sample from this study was equally small. For these reasons, the group of nurses were considered the most appropriate normative comparison for both abused and abusive lesbians.

The scores of the lesbians who abused their partners, though low, were all < 2 standard deviations from the normative groups and were also significantly lower on several interpersonal dimensions than the normative groups. Expressed inclusion (eI) and wanted inclusion (wI) were significantly lower than the norms ($t = -2.834, p = .013$ and $t = -2.070, p = .031$, respectively). Both expressed affection (eA) and wanted affection (wA) were also significantly lower than the normative samples ($t = -2.203, p = .045$ and $t = -3.424, p = .004$, respectively). Not surprisingly, the sum of wanted and expressed inclusion (ΣI) and the sum of wanted and expressed affection (ΣA) were also significantly lower ($t = -2.751, p = .016$ and $t = -3.477, p = .004$, respectively). The total of the difference scores (d) while not significantly higher ($t = 2.010, p = .064$) indicated a trend in this direction. The sum of all wanted scores (wΣ) was significantly lower ($t = -3.524, p = .003$). Finally, the grand sum of all inclusion, control, and affection scores (Σ) for abusive lesbians was significantly lower than the comparable normative score ($t = -3.007, p = .009$).

Using one-sample *t* tests for each mean, mean scores from the group of lesbians who abused their partners were also compared to the mean scores of heterosexual men who abused their female partners (Allen et al., 1989). Lesbian abusers evidenced no significant differences from heterosexual men who abused their female partners on any of the interpersonal dimensions. In fact, the scores on wanted control (wC) were virtually identical (see Table 1).

Using a *t* test for independent samples, mean scores of the lesbians who had abused their partners were also compared to the mean scores of the lesbians who had been abused. The scores were significantly different on the scale measuring differences between expressed and wanted control (dC; $t = -2.066, p = .049$). Abused lesbians scored lower than abusive lesbians on this dimension.

TABLE 1. Means and Standard Deviations for the Study Sample of Lesbians Who Abuse and Two Normative Samples of Batterers[a] and Nurses[b]

FIRO-B Scale	Lesbians Who Abused (A) N = 15		Batterers (B) N = 100			Nurses (C) N = 16		
	M	SD	M	SD	t(A vs. B)	M	SD	t(A vs. C)
Inclusion Expressed	3.20	2.60	3.10	2.00	0.15	5.10	1.90	−2.83*
Inclusion Wanted	2.53	3.34	1.90	2.80	0.74	4.60	3.37	−2.40*
Control Expressed	3.33	2.77	2.90	2.40	0.61	3.00	1.87	0.47
Control Wanted	4.20	2.31	4.20	2.90	0.00	5.00	1.84	−1.34
Affection Expressed	3.07	2.34	2.80	2.30	0.44	4.40	2.57	−2.20*
Affection Wanted	3.67	2.53	3.20	2.70	0.72	5.90	2.55	−3.42**
Summed Inclusion	5.67		5.00		0.46	9.70		−2.75*
Summed Control	7.53		7.10		0.42	8.00		−0.45
Summed Affection	6.73		6.00		0.72	10.30		−3.48**
Inclusion Difference	0.73		1.20		−0.90	0.50		0.45
Control Difference	−0.87		−1.30		0.54	−2.00		1.41
Affection Difference	−0.60		−0.40		−0.27	−1.50		1.24
Total Difference	−0.73		−0.50		−0.21	−3.00		2.01
Sum of Expressed	9.60		8.80		0.55	12.50		−2.01
Sum of Wanted	10.33		9.30		0.71	15.50		−3.52**
Grand Sum	19.93		18.10		0.68	28.00		−3.01**

[a]Allen, Calsyn, Fehrenbach, & Benton, 1989. [b]Schutz, 1978.
*p < .05; **p < .01

Finally, the mean scores of the abused lesbians were compared to the normative groups of nurses and teachers. All scores were within one standard deviation of the mean for the normative groups. Although they generally revealed no significant differences from the normative groups, abused lesbians scored significantly lower than the nurses on two scales, ΣA ($t = -2.36$, $p = .038$) and Σe ($t = -2.72$, $p = .020$), and showed a trend toward significance on two other scales, eC ($t = -2.11$, $p = .059$); wA ($t = -2.17$, $p = .053$; see Table 2).

DISCUSSION

The results of this study demonstrated support for the hypothesis that the mean scores of lesbians who had abused their partners would be measurable by

TABLE 2. Means and Standard Deviations for the Study Sample of Lesbians Who Were Abused and One Normative Sample of Nurses[a]

FIRO-B Scale	Lesbians Who Were Abused (D)		Nurses (C)		T(D vs. C)
	N = 12		N = 16		
	M	SD	M	SD	
Inclusion Expressed	4.33	2.31	5.10	1.90	−1.15
Inclusion Wanted	3.25	3.25	4.60	3.37	−1.44
Control Expressed	2.08	1.51	3.00	1.87	−2.11
Control Wanted	5.58	3.00	5.00	1.84	0.67
Affection Expressed	3.17	2.12	4.40	2.57	−2.01
Affection Wanted	4.67	1.97	5.90	2.55	−2.17
Summed Inclusion	7.58		9.70		−1.54
Summed Control	7.67		8.00		−0.36
Summed Affection	7.83		10.30		−2.36*
Inclusion Difference	1.08		0.50		0.67
Control Difference	−3.50		−2.00		1.48
Affection Difference	−1.50		−1.50		0.00
Total Difference	−3.92		−3.00		−0.68
Sum of Expressed	9.58		12.50		−2.72*
Sum of Wanted	13.50		15.50		−1.18
Grand Sum	23.08		28.00		−1.98

[a]Shutz, 1978.
*$p < .05$; **$p < .01$

an instrument designed to assess normal everyday interpersonal functioning. Further, results yielded both similarities to and differences from normative samples in everyday interpersonal functioning. While the results disconfirmed the predicted difference from the normative sample in expressed or wanted control scores, a significant difference emerged that still indicated a need for control. Specifically, even though both tested within normal limits, the functional interpersonal style of lesbians who had abused their partners indicated a higher desire for control than lesbians who had been abused. In fact, lesbians who abused their partners evidenced scores that looked more like those of men who abused their partners than like lesbians who had been abused.

While paradoxical in terms of the original hypotheses, investigation revealed that one study also measuring batterers' interpersonal styles using the FIRO-B found similar scores on expressed or wanted control to these scores (Allen et al., 1989). In fact, comparing the mean scores of lesbians who had abused their partners to the men who abused their partners in the Allen et al. study evidenced no significant differences between lesbians who abuse and men who abuse in terms of any other interpersonal dimension measured by the FIRO-B.

Lesbians who abused their partners did score significantly lower than the normative samples on expressed and wanted inclusion and affection, which resulted in concurrently lower scores on the sums of both inclusion and affection and on the grand sum. Mean scores of the lesbians who abused their partners were significantly different from the scores of lesbians who were abused by partners in only one dimension, the extent to which they preferred to give orders, dominate, or lead rather than to be ordered, dominated, or led. Although neither of the group's scores were significantly different from the normative sample on this dimension, the abusive lesbians scored significantly higher than the abused lesbians in this element of control.

Lesbians who had been abused appeared overall to be more like the normative samples than they were different. The differences evident in their scores may be attributable to abuse. Specifically, lesbians who had been abused showed a lower than normal score on overall assertiveness and a wish not to get emotionally involved. Further, their lower scores on expressed control together with moderate scores on wanted control indicated a tendency to subordinate themselves and yet worry about the implications of this subordination for their ability to assume adult responsibilities (Schutz, 1978).

Implications

Clinical implications. The findings from this study suggest that lesbians who abuse their partners are more likely to be uncomfortable with both contact and closeness than the norm. People with this interpersonal style in terms of inclusion tend not only to avoid including themselves in association or connection, but are unlikely to accept invitations from others to join in. They report that they prefer to be alone, but Schutz (1978) and Ryan (1989) contend there is more behind this. It appears that the greatest fears of people with this profile usually revolve around abandonment. Subsequently, behind the reportedly preferred self-sufficiency are feelings of loneliness and isolation, as well as anger and hostility about being excluded or abandoned. Lesbians with these scores are likely to wait for others to initiate contact or affection, yet may reject it. They report they do not want to be included, but secretly fear being abandoned enough to exist alone, avoiding even the possibility of "enmeshment."

The scores on the affection dimension also suggest that lesbians who abuse prefer more interpersonal distance in relationships. They tend to maintain emotional distance as in formalized or business-like relationships and are uncomfortable expressing affection or tenderness. People with this interpersonal preference are cautious about initiating emotional closeness lest they be rejected or perceived to be unlovable or bad. The result is that they may wait for others to initiate contact or closeness or may make "preemptive strikes" to reject or avoid others first. At best, they are highly selective about those with whom they will allow closeness; at worst, they push others away.

These preferences in terms of contact and closeness seem to suggest limited tolerance for inclusion by others as well as a limited ability to include others. They also indicate a limited ability to express affection as well as a limited wish to have others be affectionate toward them. Together, these preferences result in a stronger than normal desire not to have others initiate and yet to wait for others to initiate contact and closeness.

Interpersonal implications. Comparing the lesbians who abused to the lesbians who had been abused resulted in only one significant difference. The difference in their dC scores indicated that the abusers were significantly more likely than the victims/survivors to want to dominate rather than to subordinate themselves. This is consistent with the original hypotheses of this study and reflects a critical difference between lesbians who abuse and lesbians who are abused. This difference may also facilitate understanding an interpersonal dynamic that could develop between the lesbian who abuses and her partner. If the lesbian who abuses needs to control interpersonal distance, to lead rather than to follow, and to be very selective about who gets close in order to avoid confronting her fears of rejection or abandonment, it is likely that she will select her partner rather than the reverse. Being both undersocial and underpersonal, she may well look for and find appealing a woman for whom interaction and contact is no problem. If the prospective partner is genuinely interested in others, the abuser may reason that she may also be interested in including someone hesitant to include herself. The partner is unlikely to want to dominate and more likely to yield to the interpersonal control to preserve her safety. The lesbian who abuses may subsequently envision maintaining the interpersonal control over closeness and enmeshment that she needs to feel comfortable. However, as the prospective partner appears either to prefer or to have learned to avoid intimacy or distance, the relationship between them is soon doomed to a thin and rigid line between closeness and distance and even more consistent fears on the part of the lesbian who abuses that she is being rejected or abandoned. The lesbian who abuses, then, may actually project her own worst interpersonal fears and fulfill her own prophecy through her abuse.

Therapeutic implications. If this individual interpersonal style and the projected interpersonal dynamic are replicated in future studies with lesbians who abuse, the implications for therapy are clear. In addition to learning behavioral controls to avert abuse, the lesbian who abuses must learn to tolerate contact and intimacy without abuse or she must learn to distance without abuse. In order to select another partner who, although more threatening initially, can reciprocate sufficiently to maintain a collaborative connection, she must learn these interpersonal skills.

These findings suggest that therapy focused only on developing plans to control abusive impulses or managing anger as a means of stopping abuse will not adequately address underlying interpersonal limitations associated with intimacy and inclusion. Certainly, cognitive and behavioral controls are necessary for the safety of lesbian partners and for the self-esteem and personal accountability of the abusers. As those who work with abusive clients know well, cognitive and behavioral controls while crucial and immediate, are not sufficient to ensure long-term, integrated change (Edleson & Tolman, 1992; Hamberger, 1996). Neither should interpersonal concerns about intimacy or inclusion supplant personal accountability or an understanding of the role of internalized sexism and homophobia in perpetrating the abuse. Rather, these findings suggest that therapies for lesbians who abuse should integrate an emphasis on more adaptive interpersonal skills to undergird changes in abusive behavior.

The FIRO-B may also prove useful in identifying and customizing individualized plans in therapy for abusers. Particularly because it is not pathologically oriented, the FIRO-B may provide a brief, resonant, but less threatening assessment of interpersonal skill functioning. As with any client, a lesbian who feels both understood and not threatened or shamed by a therapist is less likely to terminate therapy prematurely. In the case of abusive clients, minimizing the risks of unnecessary interpersonal threat or premature termination means minimizing the risk of continued danger to another.

Theoretical implications. The dynamic presented through understanding the interpersonal styles of the lesbian who abuses may be interpreted for more than its value in understanding one individual or how she may construct one relationship. How does the lesbian who abuses come to be uncomfortable with contact and closeness and use abuse to control the emotional distance in a relationship? To the extent that her interpersonal style may be the result of internalized homophobia or misogyny, even individualized treatment of interpersonal skill deficiencies may not secure necessary changes. As has been found effective in therapy with a multi-faceted (Hamberger, 1996; Hamberger & Hastings, 1991) or ecological (Edleson & Tolman, 1992) approach with male abusers, feminist therapy with lesbians who abuse (Poorman & Gamache, 1985; Poorman, Gilbert, & Simmons, 1990) should also include cognitive-behavioral challenges to internalized misogyny and homophobia.

Both social milieu and interpersonal skills may operate together to support abusive behavior. Group therapies are the preferred approach for several reasons. A group can provide a new social milieu in which abuse is not condoned as an acceptable way to address interpersonal needs (Bankovics, 1984; Edleson & Tolman, 1992). Confronting interpersonal skills limitations is also a task well-suited to a group (Yalom, 1985). As with other ecological therapies, it is important to remember that while group therapy with a feminist focus may facilitate new individual decisions and learning new interpersonal skills, it will not address the need to eliminate the social opportunities that also make lesbian abuse possible. Advocacy and training to address institutionalized sexism and homophobia and their impact in legal, mental health, and social services must accompany individual changes to hold the lesbian who abuses accountable.

Research implications. The absence of significant differences between heterosexual men who abuse and lesbians who abuse appears to suggest that regardless of gender or orientation, those who abuse women share common interpersonal skills and limitations. The profile is consistent with previous reports of fears of intimacy (Hofeller, 1983), emotional inexpressiveness (Ganley & Harris, 1978), and social isolation (Gelles, 1972) among men who abuse female partners. It may even be consistent with empirically derived typologies developed about male batterers (e.g., Hamberger & Hastings, 1991) or those developed through clinical experience with lesbian abusers, that suggest characteristics like those found in narcissistic or borderline personality disorders (Coleman, 1994). Renzetti's (1992) correlations between dependency, jealousy, power imbalance, and abuse showed that as dependency and jealousy increased, types and frequency of abuse increased and an imbalance of power increased. The present findings may be consistent with, but also extend, this understanding by describing the everyday functional style and preferences of lesbian abusers and explicating a plausible dynamic by which abuse is used to control interpersonal distance.

Implications for feminist and individualist approaches. Some have viewed the fact of same-sex abuse as reason enough to reevaluate a sociopolitical explanation of abuse (Dutton, 1998; Island & Letellier, 1991). They will certainly find it compelling to interpret these findings as equally problematic. However, far from gender-neutrality or negating the feminist sociopolitical understanding of misogyny as the root of violence against women, these findings may actually suggest that internalized misogyny and homophobia play an important role in woman abuse irrespective of the gender of the perpetrator. Future research that includes assessments of internalized misogyny and homophobia could allow for more precise analysis of the relationship of these factors to abuse.

Contrary to expectations, when compared to normative samples, the lesbians who abused their partners showed not only lower levels of wanted control, but of expressed control as well. Not surprisingly, their mid-range score on wanted control implies that lesbians who abuse would not want to be controlled by others, nor have others decide for them, nor would they want to be dominated by others. The expressed control scores also seem to indicate that lesbian abusers do not feel comfortable in taking a leadership role, assuming responsibility for decision-making, or dominating others. However, scores on control within the middle range and not significantly different from the normative sample do not indicate the absence of control issues in the interpersonal styles of lesbian abusers. Lesbians who abused their partners were still significantly different from victims/survivors in their preference to control rather than to be controlled.

Abuse by definition indicates controlling another. However, control for its own sake may not necessarily be the direct objective. Rather, these results suggest that abuse may be the means of controlling the interpersonal contact and closeness poorly tolerated by the abuser. This is consistent with clinical, anecdotal evidence from the same lesbians who participated in this study. Lesbians who abused perceived themselves as victims. Their perceptions were that they had repeatedly deferred and accommodated partners until, feeling disempowered, enmeshed, and ashamed, they struck out violently to establish a sense of control. This projection served to justify the abuse for the lesbian who abused. They rationalized the abuse as a mechanism of self-empowerment; a way to assert a sense of self-control to which they thought anyone should be entitled. Their abuse, however, secured more interpersonal distance than they were comfortable with. This distance resulted in escalating tension and deference on the part of the abuser to achieve a sense of closeness and so it continued. The cycle of their abuse, then, resulted in controlling their partner's perceived closeness and distance. Of course, the abuse controlled more than this. However, it is possible that the consequent distance was precisely the purpose. If so, the abuse that lesbians perpetrate may control interpersonal closeness to offset the abusers' social preferences or deficiencies in inclusion and intimacy, rather than to establish authoritarian control for its own sake or out of a sense of entitlement to dominate, as has been found among male abusers. This dynamic warrants further investigation. Is abuse in lesbian relationships preceded by times of interpersonal closeness? Are the lines demarcating "comfortable" distance established over time through the abuse? Answers to these questions would further enhance understanding of this dynamic.

Rather than supplanting the feminist analysis of abuse as a means of garnering power or control, this study may begin to explore how abuse is used to garner or maintain personal power by controlling interpersonal distance. These findings suggest that an abuser who is "willing to use whatever tools and tactics they may have to subordinate their partner may unbalance the interpersonal power as significantly as one who is physically stronger or financially wealthier" (Merrill, 1996). Future studies utilizing additional measures of personal power or control could clarify this.

Limitations and Future Directions

The sample of lesbians who took part in this study was small in number and nearly homogeneous in ethnicity. Replications with larger and more diverse samples of lesbians are needed to confirm these findings. Secondly, comparing sample data to normative data is problematic in that it is difficult to control for differences in the groups that could be related to the variable of interest, in this case abuse. Lesbian abusers, for example, differed from the normative sample in at least one other known variable (i.e., orientation) other than being abusive. There may be other dimensions (e.g., internalized homophobia, heterosexism) along which lesbian abusers differ that account for some of the differences found in interpersonal skills. Future research should include control groups of lesbians experiencing relationship distress that does not include abuse and also control groups of lesbians in satisfying relationships. Measures of internalized homophobia and misogyny as well as measures of well-being could create a more comprehensive and clearer picture of lesbian abuse.

To date, no norms have been developed on the FIRO-B for lesbians. A large-scale study establishing normative lesbian data on the FIRO-B would not only offer additional validation to the FIRO-B and enhance the study of everyday, functional, interpersonal skills among lesbians, but could provide a useful assessment of the therapeutic needs of such subgroups of lesbians as those who are abused and those who are abusing.

More research studying lesbians who abuse is needed. To the extent that this and future studies enhance therapy for those lesbians who are actually in a position to control the abuse and its damaging effects, efforts to ensure violence-free relationships for lesbians will be improved.

NOTES

1.   All of the demographic data were self-reported by participants on a questionnaire completed prior to therapy. Responses reflected client self-definitions. Although all participants self-identified as lesbian, some responses referred to previous or current relationships with men.
2.   All 15 participants referred themselves for therapy to address their abuse of lesbian partners, although only nine self-reported abusing lesbian partners on the initial questionnaire.

REFERENCES

Allen, K., Calsyn, D. A., Fehrenbach, P. A., & Benton, G. (1989). A study of the interpersonal behaviors of male batterers. *Journal of Interpersonal Violence, 4* (1), 79-89.

Bankovics, G. (1984). *Working with men who batter.* Minneapolis, MN: Domestic Abuse Project.

Barnett, O. W., & Hamberger, L. K. (1992). The assessment of maritally violent men on the California Psychological Inventory. *Violence and Victims, 7*(1), 15-28.

Cadsky, O., & Crawford, M. (1988). Establishing batterer typologies in a clinical sample of men who assault their female partners. *Canadian Journal of Community Mental Health, 7,* 119-127.

Caesar, P. L. (1986, August). Men who batter: A heterogeneous group. In L. K. Hamberger (Chair), *The male batterer: Characteristics of a heterogeneous population.* Symposium conducted at the 94th Annual Convention of the American Psychological Association, Washington, DC.

Caesar, P. L., & Hamberger, L. K. (1989). *Treating men who batter: Theory, practice, and programs.* New York: Springer.

Coleman, V. E. (1994). Lesbian battering: The relationship between personality and the perpetration of violence. *Violence and Victims, 9*(2), 139-152.

Dutton, D. G. (1998). *The abusive personality: Violence and control in intimate relationships.* New York: Guilford.

Edleson, J. L., & Tolman, R. M. (1992). *Intervention for men who batter: An ecological approach.* Newbury Park, CA: Sage.

Elbow, M. (1977). Theoretical considerations of violent marriages. *Social Case Work, 58,* 515-526.

Fagan, J. A., Stewart, D. K., & Hansen, K. V. (1983). Violent men or violent husbands? Background factors and situational correlates. In D. Finkelhor, R. J. Gelles, G. T. Hotaling, & M. A. Straus (Eds.), *The dark side of families: Current family violence research* (pp. 49-68). Beverly Hills, CA: Sage.

Faulk, M. (1974, July). Men who assault their wives. *Medicine, Science, and the Law,* 180-183.

Ganley, A. L., & Harris, L. (1978, August). *Domestic violence: Issues in designing and implementing programs for male batterers.* Paper presented at the meeting of the American Psychological Association, Toronto.

Gelles, R. J. (1972). *The violent home: A study of physical aggression between husbands and wives.* Beverly Hills, CA: Sage.

Gluck, G. A. (1979). The Kramer-Froehle controversy: A contribution to construct validity of the FIRO-B questionnaire. *Journal of Personality Assessment, 43,* 541-543.

Gluck, G. A. (1983). *Psychometric properties of the FIRO-B: A guide to research.* Palo Alto, CA: Consulting Psychologist.

Hamberger, L. K. (1996). Intervention in gay male intimate violence requires coordinated efforts on multiple levels. In C. M. Renzetti & C. H. Miles (Eds.), *Violence in gay and lesbian domestic partnerships* (pp. 83-91). Binghamton, NY: Harrington Park Press.

Hamberger, L. K., & Hastings, J. E. (1985, March). *Personality correlates of men who abuse their partners: Some preliminary data.* Paper presented at the meeting of the Society for Personality Assessment, Berkeley, CA.

Hamberger, L. K., & Hastings, J. E. (1986). Personality correlates of men who abuse their partners: A cross validation study. *Journal of Family Violence, 1,* 323-341.

Hamberger, L. K., & Hastings, J. E. (1988). Characteristics of male spouse abusers consistent with personality disorders. *Hospital and Community Psychiatry, 39*(7), 763-770.

Hamberger, L. K., & Hastings, J. E. (1991). Personality correlates of men who batter and nonviolent men: Some continuities and discontinuities. *Journal of Family Violence, 6,* 131-147.

Hastings, J. E., & Hamberger, L. K. (1988). Personality characteristics of spouse abusers: A controlled comparison. *Violence and Victims, 3*(1), 31-47.

Hershorn, M., & Rosenbaum, A. (1991). Over- vs. under-controlled hostility: Application of the construct to the classification of maritally violent men. *Violence and Victims, 6,* 151-158.

Hofeller, K. (1983). *Battered women, shattered lives.* Palo Alto, CA: R & E Research.

Holtzworth-Munroe, A., & Stuart, G. L. (1994). Typologies of male batterers: Three subtypes and the differences among them. *Psychological Bulletin, 116*(3), 476-497.

Island, D., & Letellier, P. (1991). *Men who beat the men who love them: Battered gay men and domestic violence.* Binghamton, NY: The Haworth Press, Inc.

Kramer, E. (1980). A contribution toward the validation of the FIRO-B questionnaire. *Journal of Projective Techniques and Personality Assessment, 31,* 80-81.

Merrill, G. S. (1996). Ruling the exceptions: Same-sex battering and domestic violence theory. In C. M. Renzetti & C. H. Miley (Eds.), *Violence in gay and lesbian domestic partnerships* (pp. 9-21). Binghamton, NY: Harrington Park Press.

Poorman, P. B., & Gamache, D. (1985). Working with lesbians who abuse their partners: A description of a group intervention model. Unpublished manuscript.

Poorman, P. B., Gilbert, L., & Simmons, S. L. (1990). Guidelines for mental health systems response to lesbian battering. In P. Elliot (Ed.), *Confronting lesbian battering* (pp. 105-118). St. Paul: Minnesota Coalition for Battered Women.

Renzetti, C. M. (1992). *Violent betrayal: Partner abuse in lesbian relationships* (1st ed.). Newbury Park, CA: Sage.

Ryan, L. R. (1989). *Clinical interpretation of the FIRO-B* (3rd ed.). Palo Alto, CA: Consulting Psychologists.

Saunders, D. G. (1992). A typology of men who batter: Three types derived from cluster analysis. *American Journal of Orthopsychiatry, 62*(2), 264-275.

Schutz, W. (1978). *FIRO Awareness Scales Manual.* Palo Alto, CA: Consulting Psychologists.

Shields, N. M., McCall, G. J., & Hanneke, C. R. (1988). Patterns of family and nonfamily violence: Violent husbands and violent men. *Violence and Victims, 3,* 83-97.

Stith, S. M., Jester, S. B., & Bird, G. W. (1992). A typology of college students who use violence in their dating relationships. *Journal of College Student Development, 33,* 411-421.

Tolman, R. M., & Bennett, L. M. (1990). A review of quantitative research on men who batter. *Journal of Interpersonal Violence, 5*(1), 87-118.

White, R. J., & Gondolph, E. W. (2000). Implications of personality profiles for batterer treatment. *Journal of Interpersonal Violence, 15*(5), 467-488.

Yalom, I. D. (1985). *The theory and practice of group psychotherapy* (3rd ed.). New York: Basic Books.

Domestic Violence
in Lesbian Relationships

Diane Helene Miller
Kathryn Greene
Vickie Causby
Barbara W. White
Lettie L. Lockhart

SUMMARY. Increasingly, therapists and researchers have focused attention on domestic violence in lesbian relationships. To date, however, most research has described the incidence and types of physical violence and abuse. The present study sought to explore predictors of domestic violence in lesbian relationships. Lesbian participants filled out a survey measuring physical violence and physical aggression as well as relational and personality variables. Results indicated that lesbians do report some degree of domestic violence, characterized more often by physical aggression than by physical violence. Physical aggression was best predicted by fusion, followed by self-esteem and independence. For physical violence, however, control was the most important predictor, followed by

Diane Helene Miller, PhD, is Degree Program Assistant in the Department of Speech Communication at the University of Georgia. Kathryn Greene, PhD, is Associate Professor in the Department of Communication at Rutgers University. Vickie Causby, PhD, is Associate Professor in the School of Social Work at East Carolina University. Barbara W. White, PhD, is Dean and Professor of Social Work at the University of Texas–Austin. Lettie L. Lockhart, PhD, is Professor of Social Work at the University of Georgia.

Address correspondence to: Diane Miller, 132 Terrell Hall, Dept. of Speech Communication, University of Georgia, Athens, GA 30602 (E-mail: dmiller@arches. uga.edu).

[Haworth co-indexing entry note]: "Domestic Violence in Lesbian Relationships." Miller et al. Co-published simultaneously in *Women & Therapy* (The Haworth Press, Inc.) Vol. 23, No. 3, 2001, pp. 107-127; and: *Intimate Betrayal: Domestic Violence in Lesbian Relationships* (ed: Ellyn Kaschak) The Haworth Press, Inc., 2001, pp. 107-127. Single or multiple copies of this article are available for a fee from The Haworth Document Delivery Service [1-800-342-9678, 9:00 a.m. - 5:00 p.m. (EST). E-mail address: getinfo@haworthpressinc.com].

107

independence, self-esteem and fusion. Implications and directions for future research are discussed. *[Article copies available for a fee from The Haworth Document Delivery Service: 1-800-342-9678. E-mail address: <getinfo@haworthpressinc.com> Website: <http://www.HaworthPress.com> © 2001 by The Haworth Press, Inc. All rights reserved.]*

KEYWORDS. Battering, domestic violence, fusion, lesbians, violence, lesbian relationships

Since the 1970s, the battered women's movement has made tremendous strides in analyzing and addressing issues surrounding domestic violence. From a political context in which the problem of battered women was rarely even discussed, a movement of grassroots activism emerged that subsequently spawned an organized national and international movement. Nevertheless, this movement has been limited in some crucial ways. In particular, the issue of domestic violence in lesbian relationships has been almost entirely ignored (Ristock, 1997), both in academic analyses and in the establishment of social services for battered women. Ironically, although many founders of the battered women's movement were lesbians, the issue of battering between women often remains deeply buried, ignored or denied by heterosexual women and lesbians alike (Renzetti, 1988; Suh, 1990).

In an effort to overcome the denial that has long surrounded the issue of lesbian domestic violence, advocates for battered lesbians often concentrate on demonstrating similarities between homosexual and heterosexual domestic violence. In drawing parallels and highlighting similarities to a recognized form of violence, activists legitimize lesbian domestic violence as "real" abuse and validate the experience of its victims (Irvine, 1984; Kaye/Kantrowitz, 1992). However, some researchers and advocates propose that the next step in investigating the specificity of lesbian battering is to delineate its dynamics as a female-female problem in order to define the ways in which this phenomenon challenges our established understandings of domestic violence as a male-female problem (Hammond, 1989; Irvine, 1984). Although Carlson (1992) argues that the similarities between heterosexual and lesbian domestic violence are more significant than the differences, such a conclusion seems premature, given that the intention of much existing research has been precisely to establish such similarities.

This article reviews the existing literature on lesbian battering and provides an overview of the extent of violence reported in lesbian relationships. It generates a research question about the frequency of battering along with several hypotheses about correlates of battering in lesbian relationships. This study seeks to identify predictors of violence in lesbian relationships based on a survey measuring physical violence and physical aggression as well as relational and personality variables.

LESBIAN BATTERING

The recognition that women batter challenges an analysis of heterosexual domestic violence that links male socialization with violence. Since its inception, the battered women's movement has conceptualized the problem of domestic violence in terms of a male-female phenomenon, linking violent behavior to male gender roles and identifying the ways in which men's violence towards women is not only tolerated but actually encouraged by Western society. Acknowledging that women also perpetrate intimate violence raises new questions that illuminate the partiality of existing theoretical constructions of the problem (Hammond, 1989) and challenges some deeply-rooted cultural beliefs about women (Irvine, 1984).

Hart (1986) defines lesbian battering as "that pattern of violent and coercive behaviors whereby a lesbian seeks to control the thoughts, beliefs or conduct of her intimate partner or to punish the intimate for resisting the perpetrator's control over her" (p. 173). The scope of lesbian battering encompasses "the pattern of intimidation, coercion, terrorism or violence, the sum of all past acts of violence and the promises of future violence, that achieves enhanced power and control for the perpetrator over her partner" (Hart, 1986, p. 174). Thus the term "lesbian battering," like the broader term "domestic violence," encompasses a range of abuse that may include verbal, emotional, psychological, physical, sexual, economic and other forms of violence perpetrated by an individual on her intimate partner.

Frequency of Abuse in Lesbian Relationships

Although lesbian relationships are often presumed to be free from the power dynamics fueled by sexism and misogyny that often plague heterosexual couples (Shapiro, 1991), research does not support this conclusion. Loulan (1987) reports that among lesbians who had experienced abuse (defined in her study as verbal harassment, physical harassment, rape and/or beating) in their adult lives, 13% had been abused by a female friend or lover and 4% by a female mate. Lie and Gentlewarrier (1991) report that in their non-random, self-selected sample of lesbians, 51% reported experiencing some form of abuse (verbal, emotional, psychological, physical and/or sexual) by a female partner, and 30% reported abusing a female partner.

A study of sexual coercion in gay and lesbian relationships found that 31% of lesbians reported being the victims of forced sex perpetrated by their current or most recent partner (Waterman, Dawson, & Bologna, 1989). Sarantakos (1996) found that 17% of gays and lesbians reported violence in their relationships. Brand and Kidd (1986), in a frequently cited study, found that within heterosexual dating relationships 19% of women reported physical abuse, compared to 5% who reported physical abuse in lesbian dating relationships. However, on other measures no significant differences were found: 25% of lesbians and 27% of heterosexual women reported physical abuse in committed relationships, while 7% of lesbians and 9% of heterosexual women reported completed rape in dating relationships.

There are no reliable statistics on the actual number of lesbians who are battered each year (Carlson, 1992; Hammond, 1986; Ristock, 1991), and researchers disagree on how commonly lesbian domestic violence occurs. Although most workers within the movement estimate that battering takes place approximately as often in lesbian relationships as it does in heterosexual relationships (Carlson, 1992; S. K., 1988; Ventura, 1995), some researchers have argued that domestic violence occurs less often in lesbian relationships than among their heterosexual counterparts (Morrow & Hawxhurst, 1989). Few actual estimates of the number of battered lesbians are available, although Nealon (1992) places the number at 50,000 to 100,000 a year, and The Family Violence Project, a counseling and legal advocacy organization in San Francisco, estimates "conservatively" that one in five lesbians is battered (Ventura, 1995). Regardless of the accuracy of particular statistics, it is clear that violence does occur within some and possibly many lesbian relationships (Ristock, 1991). Thus, our research question asks:

> RQ: How frequent is physical violence in lesbian relationships in a non-clinical population?

Reasons for Violence in Lesbian Relationships

Although some causes of lesbian battering may be similar to those responsible for heterosexual battering, researchers also suggest the need to identify differences in the dynamics of power responsible for violence between women. Lesbians lack the culturally assigned power available to men, and their oppression–particularly the effects of internalized misogyny and homophobia–may be more significant than power in accounting for lesbian battering (Kelly, 1986; Ristock, 1991). The intersection of external and internalized forms of misogyny and homophobia may combine to present a multifaceted challenge to the survival and flourishing of lesbian relationships.

Control. In order to understand why an individual might resort to violence against her intimate partner, it is crucial to examine what is accomplished through such behavior. Individuals who repeatedly choose violent behavior often believe at some level that it is an effective means of achieving a desired outcome. As researchers have suggested in the case of heterosexual battering, violence is most frequently employed as a tactic for achieving "interpersonal power" or control over one's partner (Carlson, 1992; Dutton & Starzomski, 1997; Edgington, 1989; Lie & Gentlewarrier, 1991; Morrow & Hawxhurst, 1989; Ristock, 1991; Ventura, 1995; Zemsky, 1988). Dependency has been found to be correlated with abuse (Alvi & Selbee, 1997; Ellis & Dekeseredy, 1989), and some researchers report that perceived loss of power or control may also lead to increased violence (Allen & Straus, 1980; Phillips, 1988).

The alienation and isolation imposed by internalized and external oppression may construct loss of control–and the need to reclaim it–as a central concern for lesbians (Schilit, Lie, Bush, Montagne, & Reyes, 1991). Lesbians may be denied control over numerous aspects of their lives. If a lesbian is open about her sexual orientation, she may lose her family, friends, children, job, housing, and any number of other privileges she previously took for granted. She may be unable to control others' attitudes towards her or to limit the kinds of discrimination she faces as a result. Yet if she remains "in the closet" she is also denied control, subject to continuous self-monitoring and considerable added stress in an ongoing effort to conceal her identity and her intimate relationships from the eyes of others. Given the degree of control removed from lesbians in other areas of their lives, it is hardly surprising that they may feel a strong need to exercise authority in those areas where it remains within their power to do so (Burch, 1987). Based on this suggestion, the following hypothesis is proposed:

> H1: Lesbians who report a greater need for control will report more frequent use of violent tactics in conflicts with their partners.

Fusion. The concept of "merging" or "fusion" has been used to explain the genesis of both intimacy and conflict in lesbian relationships. Initially characterized as pathological (Krestan & Bepko, 1980), the phenomenon of fusion has more recently been discussed as an adaptive response to a hostile environment (Mencher, 1997; Rotenberg, 1989). In this light, fusion can be seen as a mode of resistance to the dominant culture's attempts to negate or sever the bonds of love between two women.

Krestan and Bepko (1980) borrowed and adapted the term "fusion" to describe an interpersonal dynamic they observed regularly in lesbian relationships. Fusion was defined in its original context as "the person's state of embeddedness in, of undifferentiation within, the relational context" (Karpel, 1976, p. 67). Krestan and Bepko viewed fusion as dysfunctional, as it created an "intense anxiety over any desire for separateness or autonomy within the relationship" (Krestan & Bepko, 1980, p. 277). A more recent interpretation, however, views fusion as a strategy for maintaining a couple's boundaries amid constant threats to the integrity of the relationship (Causby, Lockhart, White, & Greene, 1995; Mencher, 1997). Rotenberg (1989) argues that the predominantly negative evaluation of merger behavior is a result of a male model of individual development that values separation over connection. Moreover, she suggests that this negative evaluation must be reexamined in the context of the oppression lesbians suffer within a homophobic society.

As an adaptive response to a hostile environment, fusion internally reinforces and protects the boundaries that are continually exposed to external threat. This alternative model suggests that rather than succumbing to pressure to end their relationship, or to an attitude of disregard that demeans it or minimizes its significance, lesbian couples affirm the seriousness of their connection by forging an even stronger bond. Faced with a lack of control over other aspects of their lives, they may vigorously exert control over the one area that still seems within their power, moving closer together for mutual affirmation and protection in the face of a homophobic world (Rotenberg, 1989).

To recognize the possible adaptive function of fusion, however, is not to deny its more problematic consequences. Lesbian fusion may foster an expectation of sympathy and sameness that is bound to be frustrated in the course of a relationship. If maintenance of the relationship depends upon, or seems to depend upon, a fierce drawing together of two into one, then any experience of difference or distance between partners may be immediately perceived as a threat (McCandlish, 1982). If all of one's emotional energy is devoted to defying societal expectations and maintaining a relationship in the face of overwhelming odds (Krestan & Bepko, 1980), then any perceived external or internal threat to that relationship may arouse desperation and even panic, provoking determined, defiant, or angry acts of resistance. Lindenbaum (1985) describes the "destructive nature" of such responses, characterizing the emotion they evoke as a "murderous rage."

Although intensity of emotion does not cause violent behavior–most people experience intense emotions at times, and most do not become violent as a result–such feelings of panic and rage create an exigency for which the use of violence is one possible response. The literature on conflict in lesbian relationships, while rarely explicit about the possibility of violence, often employs a vocabulary of vehement emotion. For example, Pearlman (1987) argues that ambivalence about and fear of female power combine with complications arising from mother-daughter relationships to create "an interconnected group of ideas that can explain what seems to be a rage-in-waiting between women" (p. 323). Based on this, hypothesis 2 proposed the following:

H2: Lesbians who report higher levels of fusion will report more frequent use of violent tactics in conflicts with their partners.

Dependency. The need to achieve a balance between separateness and connection has been identified as a fundamental task in a variety of interpersonal relationships (Hess & Handel, 1959; Levinger, 1977; Peplau, Cochran, Rook, & Padesky, 1978). The literature on heterosexual battering indicates that issues of dependency are often risk factors for spousal abuse. For example, the separation or imminent separation of heterosexual partners increases the risk of domestic violence against women (Sevier, 1997). Among lesbian couples, Kurdek and Schmitt (1986) found that reciprocal dependency was a particularly important measure of relationship quality. Peplau et al. (1978) identify two primary value orientations toward pair bonding in lesbian couples, noting that differences in these orientations can lead to conflict over independence versus dependence in lesbian relationships.

Renzetti (1992) argues that the degree of dependence on a relationship and on one's intimate partner provides one clue to the dynamics of abuse. Based on a survey of 100 women who identified themselves as victims of lesbian battering, Renzetti's (1992) analysis indicates that "the greater the respondents' desire to be independent and the greater their partners' dependency, the more likely the batterer was to inflict more types of abuse with greater frequency" (p. 34). In addition, data from her interviews with 40 of the subjects linked struggles over dependency and autonomy with incidents of battering.

Renzetti's focus on dependency as a correlate of abuse challenges a common assumption that it is the more powerful partner who is more likely to inflict abuse. In analyses of male violence, feminists have argued that men's relative power over women–a power granted them by patriarchal ideology and enforced by male privilege–creates a continuum between the more subtle means of reinforcing male dominance and the explicit use of violence as a means of controlling women. With regard to heterosexual battering, then, the license society grants men to exercise control over women makes violence an effective tool of male domination. In contrast, Renzetti's analysis indicates that the use of violence in lesbian relationships is not simply a strategy employed by the more powerful partner to gain compliance from the weaker, and that the relationship between power and violence may be more complex and contradictory than originally thought. Hence, hypothesis 3 in this study proposed the following:

> H3: Lesbians who report more frequent use of violent tactics in conflicts with their partners will report a higher level of dependency as a personality trait.

Self-esteem. Within the domestic violence literature, anecdotal accounts as well as social scientific studies suggest that low self-esteem and a negative self-image are among the qualities that characterize both perpetrators and victims of heterosexual domestic violence (Crall, 1986; Okun, 1986). The jealousy and possessiveness that are frequently linked to battering behavior are associated with problems of low self-esteem and negative self-concept (Bagley & Young, 1987; Jezl, Molidor, & Wright, 1996; Walker, 1989; White & Mullen, 1989). Some researchers (Renzetti, 1992; Kaufman Kantor & Straus, 1987) suggest that the correlation between alcohol abuse and domestic violence might be explicable through the common factor of self-esteem, where those with low self-esteem and a sense of powerlessness drink and become abusive as a means of gaining control over their partner.

Similarly, a study by Coleman (1990) focused on the relationship between status inconsistency–the discrepancy between one's achieved and ascribed status–and abuse. Coleman found that greater status inconsistency led to an increased risk of violence. Her findings suggest that if status inconsistency leads to lower self-esteem, battering behavior may serve as a means of overcoming feelings of inadequacy and loss of control. Hence, hypothesis 4 in this study proposed the following:

> H4: Lesbians who report more frequent use of violent tactics in conflicts with their partners will report a lower level of self-esteem as a personality trait.

METHOD

Sample and Procedure

Participants in the current study were self-identified lesbians who attended a large regional women's music festival held in the Southeast in 1989. Of 400 questionnaires distributed, 284 were returned, for a response rate of 70%. Each respondent was currently, or had been during the previous six months, involved in a lesbian relationship. Respondents were all female, predominantly

Caucasian, and ranged in age from 21 to 60. The present study is part of a larger study examining lesbian relationships (see Causby et al., 1995; Lockhart, White, Causby, & Isaac, 1994). Each woman completed a survey about the nature of her relationship and her experiences with violence and aggression. The survey was completed anonymously and took approximately 20 minutes to complete.

Measurement Instruments

The following variables were measured: conflict resolution tactics, fusion, control, independence and self-esteem. Copies of the instrument are available from the author.

Conflict resolution tactics. Two subscales of Straus' (1979) Conflict Tactics Scale were used to measure the nature and extent of physical aggression and physical violence used to resolve conflict. This portion of the Conflict Tactics Scale contains 11 items, and respondents used a Likert scale of 0 (never) to 6 (more than 20 times a year) to respond to how often each tactic was used as a means of conflict resolution in the past year. Higher scores indicate more frequent use of particular conflict resolution tactics. The items comprising the physical aggression subscale have been described as mild forms of physical abuse (e.g., throwing an object at a partner, pushing, shoving or slapping), and reliability was .90. The physical violence subscale carries high risk for the victim and includes kicking, hitting and beating, as well as threatening to use a knife or gun. The reliability for the violence subscale was .96.

Fusion. Fusion was measured by 14 items, seven items repeated for self and partner. On a 5-point Likert-type scale of 1 (never) to 5 (always), each respondent was asked how often she [her partner] felt the need to share recreational and social activities, felt the need to do everything together, felt the need for independent time with friends, insisted on sharing professional services, made regular phone calls to partner while at work, insisted on sharing money and clothing, and attempted mind reading as a form of communication. The reliability of these subscales was .89 for self-fusion and .90 for partner fusion, with higher scores indicating greater fusion.

Independence. Lesbians in the sample were asked to describe themselves by using a list of six personality traits reflecting independence. The 5-point Likert-type items included traits such as independent, passive and submissive. The reliability of this subscale was .82, with a higher score indicating greater independence.

Control. Items on this scale evaluated the subjects' reported need for control. The six 5-point Likert-type items included traits such as controlling and harsh. The reliability of this subscale was .83, with a higher score indicating greater need for control.

Self-esteem. Hudson's (1982) Index of Self-Esteem was designed to measure the degree or severity of a respondent's problem with self-esteem. The 25 Likert-type items included statements such as "I feel that people would not like me if they really knew me well," "I feel that I bore people," and "I feel I get pushed around more than others." The reliability was good (alpha = .93). A higher score on self-esteem indicates that the respondent has greater difficulty with or lower self-esteem.

Analyses

Data were analyzed using frequencies, correlations and stepwise multiple regressions. The level of significance was set at $p \leq .05$. Reliabilities (Cronbach's alpha) were computed for all composite scales, and all scales were unidimensional (according to factor analyses). The zero order correlation matrix is presented in Table 1.

RESULTS

The research question asked about the levels of reported physical aggression and physical violence in a non-clinical lesbian population. Results are presented in Table 2, indicating moderate reported levels of physical aggression and low levels of physical violence. Thus, reports of physical aggression were much more common than reports of physical violence.

Interestingly, about half of respondents reported some physical aggression in their relationships. These conflict tactics were, in fact, relatively common. It is also important to recognize the range of reported frequency of physical ag-

TABLE 1. Correlation Matrix for Predictors with Violence Variables

	Physical Aggression	Physical Violence
Control	.14*	.26***
Independence	.14*	.23***
Self-Esteem	.19**	.14*
Fusion	.25***	.16**
Partner's Fusion	.25***	.08

* $p < .05$
** $p < .01$
*** $p < .001$

TABLE 2. Reported Frequencies of Physical Aggression and Physical Violence

Physical Aggression	%	n	M	SD
Threatened to hit or throw something at partner	16.2	46	.45	1.23
Threw, smashed, hit, or kicked something	35.9	102	.83	1.38
Pushed, grabbed, or shoved partner	23.9	68	.51	1.14
Slapped partner	8.5	24	.16	.67
Threw something at partner	11.3	32	.23	.76
Total reporting no physical aggression in relationship	53.9	153		
Physical Violence	%	n	M	SD
Kicked, bit, or hit partner with fist	7.8	22	.16	.69
Tried to hit partner with something	4.9	14	.09	.49
Hit partner with something	6.7	19	.11	.52
Beat up partner	1.8	5	.06	.48
Threatened partner with knife or gun	2.1	6	.05	.45
Shot or cut partner with gun/knife	1.4	4	.05	.45
Total reporting no physical violence in relationship	85.9	244		

gression (18-36%). Over one-third of participants reported that they or a partner threw, smashed or hit something in the past year, and one-quarter pushed, grabbed or shoved their partner. Less common among physical aggression indicators were slapping or throwing something at a partner. Just over half of all respondents (54%) reported no incidents of physical aggression in their relationships in the past year.

For physical violence, however, reports were significantly lower overall, as might be expected. The levels of physical violence can best be described as low or rare. There were few reports, for example, of hitting a partner. The lowest frequency of reports was for threatening with a gun or knife, beating up, or shooting/cutting a partner. A high percentage (86%) of respondents did not report any physical violence in their relationship in the past year.

Hypotheses 1-4 predicted relationships between personality and relational variables and the physical aggression and physical violence conflict resolution tactics, and these were mostly supported. These correlations are presented in Table 1. Hypothesis 1 was supported, indicating that lesbians with a greater need for control reported more frequent use of violent conflict tactics. Interestingly, control was more strongly related to physical violence than physical aggression. Hypothesis 2 was also supported, indicating that lesbians who reported higher levels of fusion also reported more frequent use of violent conflict tactics. In contrast to control, fusion was more strongly related to physical aggression than physical violence. Moreover, the degree of fusion reported for oneself and one's partner equally predicted physical aggression, but not physical violence. Hypothesis 3 was not supported because the relation between independence and violence was not in the predicted direction. That is, lesbians in this study who were higher in independence (not higher in dependence, as predicted) reported greater use of both physical aggression and physical violence conflict tactics. Hypothesis 4 was supported, with lesbians lower in self-esteem reporting more violent conflict tactics. Interestingly, self-esteem was more strongly related to physical aggression than physical violence.

The patterns of the results led to interesting questions about what might predict physical violence and physical aggression in lesbians. To further explore the relationships among the variables, stepwise multiple regressions were conducted. The predictor variables included fusion (self and partner), independence, control, and self-esteem. The first regression predicted physical aggression, while the second predicted physical violence.

Regression predicting physical aggression. Three variables were found to predict physical aggression in lesbian relationships. First, fusion entered the model ($F_{(1, 244)} = 17.37$, $p < .0001$, Adj. R Square = .06; beta = .25, $t = 4.13$; $p < .001$). Second, self-esteem entered the model ($F = 12.79$, $p < .0001$, R-Square change = .03; beta = .28, $t = 4.24$; $p < .001$). Third, independence entered the model ($F = 14.23$, $p < .0001$, R-Square change = .05; beta = .26, $t = 3.95$; $p < .001$). The final model accounted for 14% of the variance in use of physical aggression, and control and partner's fusion were not significant. Thus, participants who were higher in fusion, had lower self-esteem and were more independent were more likely to report physical aggression in their relationships.

Regression predicting physical violence. Four variables were found to predict physical violence in lesbian relationships. First, control entered the model ($F_{(1, 244)} = 20.61$, $p < .0001$, Adj. R Square = .07; beta = .23, $t = 3.98$; $p < .001$). Second, independence entered the model ($F = 17.50$, $p < .0001$, R-Square change = .04; beta = .32, $t = 5.03$; $p < .001$). Third, self-esteem entered the model ($F = 16.75$, $p < .0001$, R-Square change = .04; beta = .23, $t = 3.49$; $p < .001$). Finally, fusion entered the model ($F = 14.98$, $p < .0001$, R-Square change = .03; beta = .17, $t = 2.86$; $p < .01$). The final model accounted for nearly 19% of the variance in use of physical violence, and partner's fusion was not significant (although $p = .055$). Thus, participants who were higher in fusion, had lower self-esteem, were more independent and more controlling were more likely to report physical violence in their lesbian relationships.

DISCUSSION

The present study sought to explore the issue of domestic violence in lesbian relationships. Heterosexual domestic violence has received increasing attention in the past two decades, but much less is known about violence between women. The few studies that have examined lesbian violence have not added much to our understanding of why lesbians batter and what types of lesbian relationships are most likely to use violent conflict tactics. These studies have rarely focused on identifying the personality or relational variables that lead to an increased risk of violence. Moreover, most existing research has not examined the prevalence of physical aggression versus physical violence in incidents of lesbian battering.

Results indicate clearly that lesbians experience (or report) more physical aggression (46%) than physical violence (14%). That finding, that less violence than physical aggression exists, is not surprising. A more interesting but considerably more complicated question is how these figures compare with reports from other samples. Based on these data, lesbians report a degree of physical violence in their relationships similar to that reported by heterosexual women. For example, Straus, Gelles and Steinmetz (1980) reported that 12.6% of heterosexual couples had experienced severe domestic violence, which included kicking, biting, hitting with a fist, or assault using a knife or gun. Kelly and Warshafsky (1987), using a version of the Conflict Tactics Scale with a sample of gay men and lesbians, found that a comparable 47% had used physical aggression in their relationships, although they found a much lower reported frequency (3%) of physically violent tactics. In their study, women were found to have less physically aggressive partners than did men.

There are, however, serious limitations in comparing the incidence of abuse across studies due to variabilities in measurement. The range of reported incidents of domestic violence among heterosexual couples stretches from 7% to 90% depending on the definition of abuse, type of sample used, and accuracy of reporting (Lie & Gentlewarrier, 1991). Moreover, the Conflict Tactics Scale assumes all physical aggression and violence to be of the same character, preventing participants or researchers from making a crucial distinction between battering and self-defensive behavior (Renzetti, 1989). Thus, some of what appear as instances of abuse in these data might better be classified as self-defensive behavior or retaliatory aggression (Renzetti, 1992). With these cautions in mind, our own study does seem to replicate the findings of earlier studies by

Brand and Kidd (1986), Carlson (1992), and Elliott (1996) that suggest no significant differences between lesbians and heterosexual women in the likelihood of experiencing physical abuse in the context of a committed relationship. Brand and Kidd (1986) did find that male partners in heterosexual relationships committed a greater total number of abusive acts than female partners in lesbian relationships, due largely to their higher incidence of attempted rape and of physical abuse in dating (as opposed to committed) relationships. Our findings also confirm the assertions of Brand and Kidd (1986) and Morrow and Hawxhurst (1989) that lesbians employ the same types of physical aggression and physical violence that are found in heterosexual relationships.

The patterns of correlations with indicators of violence are much as expected (except for independence), though they varied in strength (see Table 1). For physical aggression, the strongest associations were with fusion and self-esteem. That is, participants who reported more physical aggression in their relationships were higher in fusion and lower in self-esteem. For physical violence, the strongest associations were with control and independence, such that participants who reported more physical violence in their relationships had greater need for control and were more independent.

The only relationship that was not as predicted was for independence. Previous research suggests that greater dependency could lead to problems that might escalate into physical violence. In the present study, however, participants higher (not lower) in independence were more likely to report physical aggression or violence in their relationships. Perhaps independence (as measured in this study) equates more with increased resources. A woman who feels she can leave the relationship might be more likely to act impulsively, using extreme measures without regard for consequences. In contrast, an individual who feels greater dependence on her partner might hesitate before embarking on a course of action with such potentially destructive consequences for the relationship. Another possible explanation for this finding is that both independence and physical violence represent violations of traditional female gender role expectations; neither is considered a traditionally "feminine" behavior. Therefore, it may be that women who express greater independence are generally less bound by gender role expectations and so are more likely to violate the norm that prohibits women from using violence as a means of self-expression or control. Finally, it is possible that because the instrument measuring independence included items such as passive and submissive, independence as measured in this study reflects a tendency to respond with action rather than inaction when one is angry, disappointed, or hurt. In this case, the findings linking independence with abusive behavior would be more predictable.

The results for the regressions were some of the most interesting in the study. The models were able to account for nearly 20% of the variance in physical aggression and physical violence. Interestingly, the order (and thus the importance) of the predictor variables differed for the two outcomes. That is, physical aggression and physical violence are predicted by the same kinds of personality and relational variables; however, the relative importance of those variables differs. Specifically, for physical aggression, fusion was the most important variable, followed by self-esteem and independence. For physical violence, however, control was most important, followed by independence, self-esteem and finally fusion.

How do two very similar clusters of predictors yield the different outcomes of physical violence and physical aggression? One possibility is that the degree of adherence or conformity to gender roles may play a role in accounting for the differences. The behaviors encompassed by the "physical aggression" designation are more indirect expressions of anger, and as such represent a less severe violation of female socialization. Behaviors such as using verbal threats, smashing things, pushing, grabbing, shoving or slapping another person represent a type of uncontrolled emotional outburst that may not be considered entirely acceptable "feminine" behavior. However, neither does this kind of dramatic acting out cross over into the forbidden realm of the masculine. Notably, within the category of physical aggression, attempts to physically harm one's partner occur significantly less often than more indirect expressions of anger that may result in harm to property but not to persons.

In contrast, the same set of predictor variables manifested in a woman who feels less bound by traditional gender roles might cross over into the realm of physical violence. More than the vehement expression of emotion that physical aggression seems to represent, the behaviors encompassed by this category involve attempts to inflict direct physical pain or injury. Such behaviors directly and flagrantly violate the bounds of women's socialization. The difference between expressing feelings versus inflicting harm also makes sense when the relative importance of the predictors is examined. In a relationship characterized by a high degree of fusion, in which the partners are deeply enmeshed, that which harms one member of the pair bond might well be experienced as harming both. Thus, an emotional outburst that communicates feelings or garners attention without causing bodily harm might be the response of choice for a partner whose goal is to reestablish the state of merger. In contrast, a relationship in which control is a predominant concern might well foster a response that imposes physical constraints on the partner when other, more subtle or less coercive means of control have failed. These are but a few possible explanations for the disparate outcomes produced by these similar variable clusters. Further research is needed to identify additional variables that might influence the outcomes of physical aggression and violence.

Implications

For therapists working with lesbian individuals or couples, these findings have several important implications. First, they suggest that the view of fusion as a problem behavior and the perception of fusion as an adaptive response to a hostile environment may *both* be correct. Based on the findings here, one might conclude that the same fierceness and determination that serve to maintain relationships in the face of external threats may have more troublesome consequences when the threat emerges from within the relationship. Thus, when one partner perceives the other behaving in a manner that causes distance between them, she may respond with a harshness and even hostility intended, ironically, to keep the relationship intact. For the therapist working with such an individual or couple, it would be useful to explore the kinds of external threats that may initially have evoked this response, and the ways the response may have become generalized to all situations perceived as threatening to the relationship. It is particularly helpful to assist clients in exploring what they hope to accomplish through aggressive or violent behavior, and to what degree such behavior has actually been effective in achieving these ends.

Second, based on these data, low self-esteem is clearly a key factor in abusive behavior, although this finding may appear counterintuitive. Abusive individuals are often perceived as having high self-esteem, viewing themselves as superior while regarding their victims as inferior or worthless. The finding that low self-esteem is related to a greater incidence of physical aggression and violence is useful for therapists both in identifying risk factors and in understanding the dynamics of abuse. Understanding how high fusion and low self-esteem might interact in abusive behavior provides a starting point for therapists and clients to examine how relational conflict escalates into physical aggression or violence through associations between threats to security, self-doubt, anger, loss, and fear. Rather than needing to persuade an abuser that her partner is worthy of respect, therapists may find that greater change is achieved by addressing the abuser's own lack of self-respect.

Third, the finding that lesbians who report greater independence are more likely to report aggression and violence in their relationships may assist therapists in a number of ways. As suggested previously, it is possible that in this study the construct of independence reflected greater resources, and thus less regard for the consequences of aggressive or violent behavior. Alternatively, the characteristic measured here may suggest a tendency to take action to shape one's environment and other people in order to bring about desired consequences. In either case, therapists can assist clients in examining their own views about the role of independence and interdependence in intimate relationships. In particular, clients might reflect on how a sense of independence influences their expectations of their partner and of the relationship, identifying both positive and negative outcomes. Where independence represents the ability to take an active rather than passive role in addressing relational problems, therapists may help clients envision a wider range of possible responses, developing action plans that nurture rather than fracture a couple's bond.

Finally, the element of control was found to influence the incidence of physical violence, suggesting a point of intersection with studies of heterosexual domestic violence in which control is a compelling factor. As discussed earlier, however, relational control may take on a special significance among members of an oppressed minority group who are so often denied control in other areas of their lives. Therapists must be aware of the reasons control may become an overriding concern for some lesbian clients, and clients may benefit from identifying areas in their lives in which they feel the greatest and the least sense of control. Therapists may assist clients in developing a greater internal locus of control in other areas, while also considering the unwanted consequences of trying to control their partner's behavior. Finally, therapists who perceive excessively controlling behavior in one or both members of a couple, particularly if accompanied by the presence of other risk factors, may want to ask direct questions about a couple's modes of argument and their means of conflict resolution.

Limitations

Results from the present study should be interpreted with a few limitations in mind. First, reports are from only one perspective; that is, these are not couple data (not paired as such) and differences in the partners' perceptions may exist. However, the psychological and relational variables reported in the present study may best be seen from an individual perspective. The fusion measure, for example, is a good addition because it provides views of both self and other in the relationship. There is always a possibility of social desirability bias in responses, but it would be difficult to ascertain whether participants might over- or underreport domestic violence in their relationships.

Because this data is approximately ten years old, it is possible that the prevalence and types of domestic violence have changed during that time. However, it remains very difficult to gather detailed data from a nonclinical lesbian population, and good sampling and measurement should help balance time-related changes. Perhaps more importantly, this sample may not be representative of lesbians as a group. Specifically, it may overrepresent lesbians who attend visible woman-identified functions. Additionally, this particular event took place in the Southeast and participants paid a fee to attend. Thus, the lesbians in this sample are likely to disproportionately represent middle- or upper-middle class Caucasian women from the southeastern United States. Finally, not all variables were measured in the present study.

Future Research

Although this study adds to current understandings of the nature of domestic violence in lesbian relationships, there are other areas yet to be examined. Future research could include additional variables such as status and power differences, means of resolving violent disputes, availability of social support and disclosure of homosexuality. It would be particularly helpful to know what kinds of couples sought and benefited from any type of third party intervention, including counseling. It is also possible that a more systemic approach to domestic violence (a couple's perspective) might be beneficial. One study of heterosexual adolescents found 66% of adolescents in relationships with violence were mutual batterers (Gray & Foshee, 1997); it is possible that some lesbians, too, are in a system of mutual violence. Thus, we should also look more closely at how couples deal with violence.

Another important area for future research is the investigation of when and how conflict in intimate lesbian relationships escalates into physical aggression and/or violence, and when it remains in the realm of discussion or argument. By identifying instances in which couples resolve conflict through non-violent means and comparing these to incidents in which one or both partners employ physically aggressive or violent tactics, we may begin to isolate cognitive and emotional patterns of response that lead to abusive behavior. If we are able to identify how these patterns differ in violent and non-violent episodes of conflict, we may learn how to intervene earlier and more effectively in order to redirect abusive outbursts into more productive channels.

A final suggestion for future investigations is that the nature of some of the variables examined here, especially fusion, might best be seen in a longitudinal study. Predicting long-term violent outcomes would be highly beneficial, so that at-risk couples might be identified early on and interventions developed to reduce the potential for violence. The present study adds to what we know about lesbian relationships and domestic violence, but further research is urgently needed in this area.

REFERENCES

Allen, C. M., & Straus, M. A. (1980). Resources, power, and husband-wife violence. In M. A. Straus & G. T. Hotaling (Eds.), *The social causes of husband-wife violence* (pp. 188-210). Minneapolis: University of Minnesota Press.

Alvi, S., & Selbee, K. (1997). Dating status variations and woman abuse. *Violence Against Women, 3*, 610-628.

Bagley, C., & Young, L. (1987). Juvenile prostitution and child sexual abuse: A controlled study. *Journal of Community Mental Health, 6*, 5-26.

Brand, P. A., & Kidd, A. H. (1986). Frequency of physical aggression in heterosexual and female homosexual dyads. *Psychological Reports, 59*, 1307-1313.

Burch, B. (1987). Barriers to intimacy: Conflict over power, dependency, and nurturing in lesbian relationships. In Boston Lesbian Psychologies Collective (Ed.), *Lesbian psychologies: Explorations and challenges* (pp. 126-141). Urbana: University of Illinois Press.

Carlson, B. E. (1992). Questioning the party line on family violence. *Affilia, 7*, 94-110.

Causby, V., Lockhart, L., White, B., & Greene, K. (1995). Fusion and conflict resolution in lesbian relationships. *Journal of Gay & Lesbian Social Services, 3*, 67-82.

Coleman, V. E. (1990). *Violence between lesbian couples: A between groups comparison.* Unpublished doctoral dissertation, University Microfilms International, 9109022.

Crall, S. (1986). Love is not enough. In K. Lobel (Ed.), *Naming the violence: Speaking out about lesbian battering* (pp. 32-36). Seattle: Seal Press.

Dutton, D. G., & Starzomski, A. J. (1997). Personality predictors of the Minnesota power and control wheel. *Journal of Interpersonal Violence, 12*, 70-82.

Edgington, A. (1989, July 16-22). Anyone but me. *Gay Community News, 17*, 1-4.

Elliott, P. (1996). Shattering illusions: Same-sex domestic violence. *Journal of Gay & Lesbian Social Services, 4*, 1-8.

Ellis, D., & Dekeseredy, W. (1989). Marital status and woman abuse: The DAD model. *International Journal of the Sociology of the Family, 19*, 67-87.

Gray, H. M., & Foshee, V. (1997). Adolescent dating violence: Differences between one-sided and mutually violent profiles. *Journal of Interpersonal Violence, 12*, 126-141.

Hammond, N. (1986). Lesbian victims and the reluctance to identify abuse. In K. Lobel (Ed.), *Naming the violence: Speaking out about lesbian battering* (pp. 190-197). Seattle: Seal Press.

Hammond, N. (1989). Lesbian victims of relationship violence. In E. D. Rothblum & E. Cole (Eds.), *Loving boldly: Issues facing lesbians* (pp. 89-105). New York: Harrington Park Press.

Hart, B. (1986). Lesbian battering: An examination. In K. Lobel (Ed.), *Naming the violence: Speaking out about lesbian battering* (pp. 173-189). Seattle: Seal Press.

Hess, R. D., & Handel, G. (1959). *Family worlds: A psychosocial approach to family life.* Chicago: University of Chicago Press.

Hudson, W. (1982). *The clinical measurement package: A field manual.* Chicago: Dorsey Press.

Irvine, J. (1984, January 14). Lesbian battering: The search for shelter. *Gay Community News, 11*, 13-17.

Jezl, D. R., Molidor, C. E., & Wright, T. L. (1996). Physical, sexual, and psychological abuse in high school dating relationships: Prevalence rates and self esteem issues. *Child and Adolescent Social Work Journal, 13*, 69-87.

Karpel, M. (1976). Individuation: From fusion to dialogue. *Family Process, 15*, 65-82.

Kaufman Kantor, G., & Straus, M. A. (1987). The "drunken bum" theory of wife beating. *Social Problems, 34*, 213-230.

Kaye/Kantrowitz, M. (1992). *The issue is power.* San Francisco: Aunt Lute Books.

Kelly, E. E., & Warshafsky, L. (1987, July). Partner abuse in gay male and lesbian couples. Paper presented at the Third National Conference for Family Violence Researchers, Durham, NH.

Kelly, L. (1986). National coalition against domestic violence. *off our backs, 1*, 4-5.

Krestan, J. A., & Bepko, C. S. (1980). The problem of fusion in the lesbian relationship. *Family Process, 19*, 277-289.

Kurdek, L. A., & Schmitt, J. P. (1986). Relationship quality of partners in heterosexual married, heterosexual cohabiting, and gay and lesbian relationships. *Journal of Personality and Social Psychology, 51*, 711-720.

Levinger, G. (1977). Re-viewing the close relationship. In G. Levinger & H. Rausch (Eds.), *Close relationships: Perspectives on the meaning of intimacy.* Amherst, MA: University of Massachusetts Press.

Lie, G. Y., & Gentlewarrier, S. (1991). Intimate violence in lesbian relationships: Discussion of survey findings and practice implications. *Journal of Social Science Research, 15*, 41-59.

Lindenbaum, J. P. (1985). The shattering of an illusion: The problem of competition in lesbian relationships. *Feminist Studies, 11*, 85-103.

Lockhart, L. L., White, B. C., Causby, V., & Isaac, A. (1994). Letting out the secret: Violence in lesbian relationships. *Journal of Interpersonal Violence, 9*, 469-492.

Loulan, J. (1987). *Lesbian passion: Loving ourselves and each other.* San Francisco: Spinsters/Aunt Lute.

McCandlish, B. M. (1982). Therapeutic issues with lesbian couples. *Journal of Homosexuality, 7*, 71-78.

Mencher, J. (1997). Intimacy in lesbian relationships: A critical reexamination of fusion. In J. V. Jordan (Ed.), *Women's growth in diversity: More writings from the Stone Center* (pp. 311-330). New York: The Guilford Press.

Morrow, S. L., & Hawxhurst, D. M. (1989). Lesbian partner abuse: Implications for therapists. *Journal of Counseling and Development, 68*, 58-62.

Nealon, P. (1992, June 1). Gays, lesbians also feel domestic violence. *Boston Globe.*

Okun, L. (1986). *Woman abuse: Facts replacing myths.* Albany, NY: SUNY Press.

Pearlman, S. F. (1987). The saga of continuing clash in lesbian community, or will an army of ex-lovers fail? In Boston Lesbian Psychologies Collective (Ed.), *Lesbian psychologies: Explorations and challenges* (pp. 313-326). Chicago: University of Illinois Press.

Peplau, L. A., Cochran, S., Rook, K., & Padesky, C. (1978). Loving women: Attachment and autonomy in lesbian relationships. *Journal of Social Issues, 34*(3), 7-27.

Phillips, R. (1988). *Putting asunder: A history of divorce in western society.* Cambridge, U.K.: Cambridge University Press.

Renzetti, C. M. (1988). Violence in lesbian relationships: A preliminary analysis of causal factors. *Journal of Interpersonal Violence, 3,* 381-399.

Renzetti, C. M. (1989). Building a second closet: Third party responses to victims of lesbian partner abuse. *Family Relations, 38,* 157-163.

Renzetti, C. M. (1992). *Violent betrayal: Partner abuse in lesbian relationships.* Newbury Park, CA: Sage.

Ristock, J. L. (1991). Beyond ideologies: Understanding violence in lesbian relationships. *Canadian Woman Studies/Les Cahiers de la Femme, 12,* 74-79.

Ristock, J. L. (1997). The cultural politics of abuse in lesbian relationships: Challenges for community action. In V. Benokraitis (Ed.), *Subtle sexism: Current practices and prospects for change* (pp. 279-296). Thousand Oaks, CA: Sage.

Rotenberg, L. (1989). Impact of homophobia, heterosexism and closetedness on intimacy dynamics in lesbian relationships. *Resources for Feminist Research/Documentation sur la Recherche Feministe, 18,* 3-9.

S. K. (1988, February). Conversations on healing. *Matrix, 6.*

Sarantakos, S. (1996). Same-sex couples: Problems and prospects. *Journal of Family Studies, 2,* 147-163.

Schilit, R., Lie, G. Y., Bush, J., Montagne, M., & Reyes, L. (1991). Intergenerational transmission of violence in lesbian relationships. *Affilia, 6,* 72-87.

Sevier, A. (1997). Recent or imminent separation and intimate violence against women. *Violence Against Women, 3,* 566-589.

Shapiro, L. (1991). Lesbian battering: Romance to ruin. *off our backs,* 16-17.

Straus, M. A. (1979). Measuring intrafamilial family conflict and violence: The conflict tactics (CT) scales. *Journal of Marriage and the Family, 41,* 75-88.

Straus, M. A., Gelles, R. J., & Steinmetz, S. (1980). *Behind closed doors: Violence in the American family.* Garden City, NY: Anchor/Doubleday.

Suh, M. (1990, September/October). Lesbian battery. *Ms. Magazine, 1,* 48.

Ventura, M. J. (1995, August). Intimate abuse: Domestic violence in lesbian relationships. *Deneuve, 5,* 40-42.

Walker, L. E. (1989). *Terrifying love.* New York: Harper Perennial.

Waterman, C. K., Dawson, L. J., & Bologna, M. J. (1989). Sexual coercion in gay male and lesbian relationships: Predictors and implications for support services. *The Journal of Sex Research, 26,* 118-124.

White, G. L., & Mullen, P. E. (1989). *Jealousy: Theory, research, and clinical strategies.* New York: Guilford Press.

Zemsky, B. (1988, December 4-10). Lesbian battering: A challenge to our community. *Gay Community News, 16,* 1.

Index

abandonment, feelings of
    by lesbians who abuse, 97-98
ableism, 12
accountability
    effect of, 3
    morality and, 4
ageism, 12
anger, 11
anti-Semitism, 12

Balsam, Kimberly F., 25
Battered Woman Questionnaire
    (BWQ), 46-47
battering
    defined, 40
    See also lesbian battering; lesbian
        domestic abuse
borderline personality disorder, 89
    of abusers, 13,15,17,100
BWQ (Battered Woman Question-
    naire), 46-47

California Personality Inventory
    (CPI), 89
causation theories
    future research on, 18-19
    literature regarding, 14-16
"chosen family"
    support from, 2-3
classism
    power inequity in, 2,43
    "triple jeopardy" faced by, 12
Cleaver, Richard, 81-82

clinical interventions
    couples counseling, safety issues and,
        55
    homophobic "coming out" control
        and, 54-55
    isolation, empowering against, 54-55
    minimization of violence myth and,
        55-56
    outside resource familiarity and, 55
    re-victimization by, 55
    safety issues and, 54
co-dependency fictions, 13-14
"coming out"
    to health-care providers, fear of,
        52-53
    homophobic control and, 32,41
    relationship affected by, 2
    safety issues and, 3-4
community
    community silence and, 44-45
    image protection need and, 34
    lesbian battering denial in, 33-34
    lesbians of color as, 12
    See also community intervention;
        lesbian community
community intervention
    barriers to, 11
    buildings coalitions in, 19
    future directions in, 19
    homophobia barriers to, 44
    for lesbians of color, 53-54
    racism barrier to, 44
    utopia myths and, 44-45
compulsive personality disorder, 89
Conflict Tactics Scale, 10,115,119
control
    abuser as victim and, 101
    alienation from oppression and, 111

degree of aggression and, 3
homophobic "coming out" power
    and, 54-55
of interpersonal distance, 101-102
mutual battering and, 52
as predictor of lesbian domestic
    violence
    aggression *vs.* violence and,
        116*table*,117-118,120
    measurement of, 115-116
    therapeutic implications re-
        garding, 123
    vs. dependency as violence pre-
        dictor, 112-113
couples assessment technique, 61
couples counseling
    safety issue in, 13,14,55
    See also feminist counselors,
        decentering heterosexuality
        by
CPI (California Personality Inven-
    tory), 89
criminal justice system
    barriers to intervention within,
        11-12
    effectiveness of, 14
    heterosexism in, 51-52
    homophobia in, 14,17,51
    patriarchal characteristics of, 18
    perceptions, role of in, 16

decision factor
    for abuse to occur, 15
dependency
    aggression *vs.* violence and,
        116*table,* 120
    in hetero *vs.* homosexual domestic
        abuse, 113
    measurement of, 115
    power *vs.* violence relationship
        and, 113-114
depression
    internalized homophobia and, 29,
        30-31

destruction of property
    prevalence of, 10
discrimination, elements of, 75
domestic abuse
    defined, 74
    See also lesbian battering; lesbian
        domestic abuse; predictors of
        domestic violence

ecological intervention model
    causal factors and, 15-16
education
    importance of, 4-5
emotional abuse, 40
    isolation, 54-55
emotional inexpressiveness, 100
emotional-psychological abuse
    characteristics of, 11
    prevalence of, 9,10
ethnicity
    power inequity in, 2
expressed affection (eA) needs, 92,93,
    94,95*table*,96*table*
expressed control (eC) needs, 92,93,
    94,95*table*,96*table*
expressed inclusion (eI) needs, 92,93,
    94,95*table*,96*table*

family members, support of
    relationship affected by, 2
    See also "chosen family"
Family Violence Project, 110
feminism
    domestic violence dynamics and, 8
    See also feminist counselors,
        decentering heterosexuality by
feminist counselors, decentering hetero-
    sexuality by
    counseling preference of abused and,
        60-61
    focus group discussions

affirmation and disruption fa-
cilitation of, 61
consensual sadomasochism,
68-69
discourse analysis of, 61,63
dominant feminist discourses,
63-66
heterosexist normative frameworks and, 63
heterosexual relationships, re-
turning to, 64
marginal feminist discourses,
63,66-67
mutual abuse concept and,
65-66
naming whiteness, 67-68
results *vs.* causes emphasis
and, 65
social context of, 61
stress causing abuse and, 64
lesbian abuse literature review,
60-61
"necessary speech" concept and,
63,66
study conclusion, 69-70
study method, 61-62
analysis, 63
participants, 62-63
summary regarding, 59-61
"trauma talk" concept and, 63,
64-65
feminist models of battering, 42
feminist psychology
early work of, 1
FIRO-B (Fundamental Interpersonal
Relations Orientation-Be-
havior), 89,92-93,99,102
Fundamental Interpersonal Relations
Orientation-Behavior
(FIRO-B), 89,92-93,99,102
fusion, as predictor of lesbian domestic abuse
as adaptive function, 112,122
aggression *vs.* violence and,
116*table,*118,120

defined, 112
degree of aggression and, 3
of intimacy and conflict, 111
measurement of, 115
oppression of homophobic society
and, 112

gender roles
inequalities in, results of, 42
power relationships and, 43
victim-blaming, homophobia and, 35
group therapy
causal factors and, 15-16
for lesbians who abuse, 18
safety and effectiveness issues of, 18
See also couples counseling; feminist counselors, decentering
heterosexuality by
guilt
internalized homophobia and, 31

HBWQ (Heterosexual Battered Woman
Questionnaire), 47
health-care providers
"coming" out to, fear of, 52-53
culture stereotyping of, 53
heterosexism of, 53
heterosexism
core sexual shame and, 80
in the criminal justice system, 51-52
defined, 28,75
of health-care providers, 53
helping professionals, belief of, 50
heterosexual *vs.* homosexual relationships and, 42
impact of, 2
institutional heterosexism, 100
liberation theology and, 81-82
of service providers, 50,60
in shelters, 53

bia; predictors of domestic
violence
lesbian domestic abuse, literature review regarding, 8-16,60-61
anecdotal evidence, 11-12,17
community interventions, 13-16
criminal justice system responses,
16
incident characteristics, 10-11
lethality statistics, 11,16
prevalence estimates, 9-10,16-17
therapeutic interventions, 13-14
underserved populations, 12-13
lesbian relationships
power differentials in, 1-2
violence in, 2
See also heterosexism; homophobia; lesbian domestic abuse;
predictors of domestic violence
lesbians of color
as communities, 12
community coalitions involving, 19
community homophobia and, 51
health-care providers, culture stereotyping of, 53
outreach programs to, 53-54
racism against, 12-13
See also homophobia, lesbian
battering in context of; minority stress
lesbians who abuse
dependency upon partner and, 33
group therapy for, 18
individual pathology of, 13
literature regarding, 12-13
personality disorders of, 15,17
risk factors of, 17
sociopolitical factors of, 13,18-19
support groups for, 61
See also accountability; lesbians
who abuse, personality
characteristics of; predictors
of domestic violence

lesbians who abuse, personality characteristics of
abandonment issues and, 97
affection preferences and, 97-98
attachment deficiencies and, 88
behavior and social variables, links
between, 90
early family experiences and, 88
empathy deficiencies, 88
group therapy intervention and,
99-100
interpersonal skills interventions, 100
personality disorders, 88-89
research limitations and, 89-90
social skills deficiencies and, 88
study discussion, 95-97
feminist approach implications,
100-102
future directions of research, 102
interpersonal implications, 98
research implications, 100
study limitations, 102
theoretical implications, 99-100
therapeutic implications, 98-99
study method
instrument, 92-93
participants, 91-92
procedure, 93
study objectives, 90-91
study results, 93-95
summary regarding, 87-91
treatment limitations and, 89-90
See also predictors of domestic violence
liberation theology intervention model,
81-82

male privilege
effects of, 1
hierarchy and, 2
marginal feminist discourses, 63,66-67
consensual sadomasochism, 68-69
naming whiteness, 67-68
McLaughlin, Erin, 39

barriers to, 11
Society and the Healthy Homosexual
        (Weinberg), 75
sociopolitical factors
    future research on, 18-19
Steinem, Gloria, 8
support groups
    safety and effectiveness issues of,
        18

therapeutic intervention
    barriers to, 11
    efficacy of, 17
    heterosexual bias in, 13
    literature regarding, 13-14
    See also couples counseling; fem-
        inist counselors,
            decentering heterosexuality
            by
threats
    prevalence of, 10
Tigert, Leanne, 73
trauma
    defined, 76
    effects of, 76-77
"trauma talk" concept, 63,64-65
"triple jeopardy," 12
truth
    effect of, 3
truth and Reconciliation Courts of
        South Africa, 4

underserved populations
    See lesbians of color

verbal abuse
    prevalence of, 10,26
victim-blaming
    education to counter, 4-5
    gender roles, homophobia and, 35
    by therapists, 13-14
violence
    cyclical model of, 3
    keeping it personal and, 3
    See also accountability; lesbian bat-
        tering; lesbians who abuse; les-
        bians who abuse, personality
        characteristics of; perpetrator
vulnerabilities
    examples of, 10-11

wanted affection (wA) needs, 93,94,
        95*table*,96*table*
wanted control (wC) needs, 92-93,94,
        95*table*,96*table*
wanted inclusion (wI) needs, 92,93,94,
        95*table*,96*table*
WDW (Who Does What Questionnaire),
        43
Weinberg, George, 75
Who Does What Questionnaire (WDW),
        43